"The rare book that is both inspiring and immediately practical. The wisdom that Michael and Megan share is the by-product of years of work as two of the most trusted professional coaches in America. I highly recommend *Win at Work and Succeed at Life*!"

—CHRIS McCHESNEY, bestselling author, leader of execution at FranklinCovey

"Success doesn't mean sacrificing a full life, and a full life doesn't require sacrificing success. In this poignant book, Michael and Megan share strategies for the magic that happens when high achievers become fully present for their families and communities too. Highly recommended for anyone looking to win in all spheres of life."

—LAURA VANDERKAM, author of *Off the Clock* and *Juliet's School of Possibilities*

"Filled with practical and thought-provoking ideas and tools, this book will help even the busiest professional transform the tension between work and life into a true Double Win."

—JOHN C. MAXWELL, founder of The Maxwell Leadership Enterprise

"We all struggle with the time and energy demands of juggling our personal and professional lives. Michael Hyatt and Megan Hyatt Miller prove that this is not a zero-sum game. You can actually have both if you follow their clear and practical guidelines."

—JOHN TOWNSEND, PhD, *New York Times* bestselling coauthor of *Boundaries*

"A riveting and insightful how-to guide for transforming you from overwhelmed to in control. Your team will thank you—and so will your family."

—EMILY BALCETIS, author of *Clearer, Closer, Better*; associate professor of psychology at NYU

"Michael Hyatt and Megan Hyatt Miller have cracked the code to transform your productivity and your relationships. If you're looking for that 'missing piece' to get your life and time back, run—don't walk—to this book!"

—JULIE SOLOMON, host of *The Influencer Podcast*

"Practical, candid, and packed with hard-earned wisdom, *Win at Work and Succeed at Life* might just be the most comprehensive guide to a thriving life I've encountered."

—TODD HENRY, author of *The Motivation Code*

"A brilliant and timely book that finally answers the noise of #Hustle culture with insight and evidence. A clear reminder that there really is another (better) way."

—BRUCE DAISLEY, author of *Eat Sleep Work Repeat*;
former Twitter vice president for Europe,
Middle East, and Africa

"This book has the power to change the way you think and work in a profound way. Using the principles and practices that Michael and Megan have developed, you will not only win, you will find the peace of mind and satisfaction we all strive to achieve in life."

—CRAIG GROESCHEL, pastor of Life.Church;
New York Times bestselling author

"We love to work. Nothing wrong with that. But what happens when work dominates our lives? Michael and Megan expose what overwork is doing to us. (Hint: It's bad.) But they don't stop there! They share five simple practices to help busy, overwhelmed professionals like you and me experience success at the office—and in the rest of our lives as well."

—IAN MORGAN CRON, bestselling coauthor of
The Road Back to You

"Michael Hyatt and Megan Hyatt Miller have helped thousands of people tear down the barriers that keep them from finding work-life balance. Now they've distilled their experience into an accessible, thoughtful, and deeply useful book."

—ALEX SOOJUNG-KIM PANG, founder of the Restful Company; author of *Rest* and *Shorter*

"My first role in Michael's life was as his executive coach a few decades ago. And from this starting point, he and I have become close friends as he has evolved from his role as a corporate leader to a leadership-and-life thought leader. I share this because I have watched him firsthand live out the principles he and his incredibly gifted partner and daughter, Megan, outline in the pages of this fantastic book. Winning at work and succeeding at life is possible. I encourage you to grab your pen and dive into the pages that follow so you can do both."

—DANIEL HARKAVY, founder of Building Champions

"I've known Michael for decades, and every time he has something to say, I know it's going to be really helpful. This book is more proof of that—practical as always, but deep, too!"

—JOHN ELDREDGE, president of Wild at Heart; bestselling author

"We should be deeply suspicious of any approach that requires a sacrifice of family life in order to succeed at work—or vice versa. No one truly wins the game unless they win both, and this elegant book spells out how you can achieve the 'Double Win' and enjoy the process."

—RAY EDWARDS, communication strategist; author of *How to Write Copy That Sells*

"Michael Hyatt and Megan Hyatt Miller take aim at the false notion that success at work is only attained by failing at home. They point to a better way of living and working, one where winning in one area fuels the other."

—SKIP PRICHARD, president and CEO, OCLC, Inc.; *Wall Street Journal* bestselling author of *The Book of Mistakes: 9 Secrets to Creating a Successful Future*

"Not only will this book be extremely helpful to you as you seek to navigate your own Double Win, but you can be sure that, written by a dad and daughter, it has the ring of authenticity. And truth. I had the joy of watching so much of what Michael and Megan write about unfold firsthand. You're going to love this book."

—ROBERT WOLGEMUTH, bestselling author

"Here's good news: you don't have to sacrifice personal happiness for career success. If you doubt that, read Michael Hyatt and Megan Hyatt Miller's latest. This is more than a business book. It's an inspiring personal story of work-life transformation."

—BOB GOFF, bestselling author of *Love Does*

"*Win at Work and Succeed at Life* is a life-transforming read."

—PATRICK LENCIONI, CEO and founder of The Table Group; bestselling author of *The Five Dysfunctions of a Team* and *The Advantage*

WIN
AT WORK
and
SUCCEED
AT LIFE

WIN AT WORK
and
SUCCEED AT LIFE

5 PRINCIPLES *to* FREE YOURSELF
FROM *the* CULT *of* OVERWORK

MICHAEL HYATT *and*
MEGAN HYATT MILLER

BakerBooks

a division of Baker Publishing Group
Grand Rapids, Michigan

© 2021 by Michael Hyatt and Megan Hyatt Miller

Published by Baker Books
a division of Baker Publishing Group
PO Box 6287, Grand Rapids, MI 49516-6287
www.bakerbooks.com

Printed in the United States of America

Library of Congress Cataloging-in-Publication Data
Names: Hyatt, Michael S., author. | Hyatt Miller, Megan, 1980– author.
Title: Win at work and succeed at life : 5 principles to free yourself from the cult of overwork / Michael Hyatt and Megan Hyatt Miller.
Description: Grand Rapids, Michigan : Baker Books, a division of Baker Publishing Group, [2021]
Identifiers: LCCN 2020052222 (print) | LCCN 2020052223 (ebook) | ISBN 9780801094699 (cloth) | ISBN 9781540900975 (paperback) | ISBN 9781493428700 (ebook)
Subjects: LCSH: Work-life balance. | Success. | Work-life balance—Religious aspects—Christianity. | Success—Religious aspects—Christianity.
Classification: LCC HD4904.25 .H934 2021 (print) | LCC HD4904.25 (ebook) DDC 650.1—dc23
LC record available at https://lccn.loc.gov/2020052222
LC ebook record available at https://lccn.loc.gov/2020052223

Some names and identifying details have been changed to protect the privacy of individuals.

The authors are represented by Alive Literary Agency, 7680 Goddard Street, Suite 200, Colorado Springs, CO 80920, www.aliveliterary.com

21 22 23 24 25 26 27   7 6 5 4 3 2 1

CONTENTS

1. The Double Win   11

2. The Cult of Overwork   29

3. Our Multifaceted Lives
   - ▶ PRINCIPLE 1: Work Is Only One of Many Ways to Orient Your Life   51
   - ▶ DOUBLE WIN PRACTICE: Define Your Own Double Win   71

4. Liberation through Limits
   - ▶ PRINCIPLE 2: Constraints Foster Productivity, Creativity, and Freedom   75
   - ▶ DOUBLE WIN PRACTICE: Constrain Your Workday   90

5. The Promise of Balance
   - ▶ PRINCIPLE 3: Work-Life Balance Is Truly Possible   95
   - ▶ DOUBLE WIN PRACTICE: Schedule What Matters   113

6. A Profitable Pause

▸ PRINCIPLE 4: There's Incredible Power in Nonachievement   117

▸ DOUBLE WIN PRACTICE: Maintain a Hobby That Delights You   134

7. Rethinking Sleep

▸ PRINCIPLE 5: Rest Is the Foundation of Meaningful, Productive Work   139

▸ DOUBLE WIN PRACTICE: Start the Day with a Good Night's Sleep   153

8. Creating Your Own Double Win   159

Notes   177

Thanks   191

Index   195

THE DOUBLE WIN

The really tough choices . . . are genuine dilemmas
because each side is firmly rooted in one of our basic,
core values.

RUSHWORTH KIDDER[1]

Her tears were born out of years of silent suffering.
Each drop carried a memory fed from a deep well
of hurt. Sitting next to my wife, Gail, in our family den, I (Michael) was caught totally off guard. I felt as
though there weren't enough tissues in the world to wipe
away the pain.

Gail and I have been married for more than forty years.
She's always been my biggest supporter and cheerleader. But
that afternoon silent resentment and regret finally bubbled
over. I wanted to defend myself. Thankfully, I somehow had
the presence of mind to keep my mouth shut long enough
to listen.

Several hours earlier, I'd been sitting with my boss in his spacious C-suite office at Thomas Nelson Publishers. The walls were lined with books our company had published. I felt proud scanning the upright spines. After all, my team and I had produced a bunch—including several bestsellers—all while transforming the company's worst-performing division into its top profit generator.

But the CEO had called me in for more than an attaboy. He reached across the desk and handed me the biggest bonus check I'd ever seen. I had to read the number twice. It was larger than my annual salary! I somehow resisted the overpowering urge to call Gail with the news. I wanted to tell her in person. I knew she'd be elated.

The two of us had an unspoken, unarticulated pact, going back to our earliest years together. Here's how it went, more or less: We've got a big family, five kids with lots of expenses. I will go work and do whatever's needed to provide for us. Meanwhile, Gail will manage the home front. We'll check in occasionally, but we'll stay in our lanes.

Off we went in separate directions, me to work, Gail to running the home. My career was pretty much everything for me then, and Gail frequently found herself covering for me with the kids while I worked nights and weekends. She never complained behind my back about my absence. Quite the opposite. "I know Dad wishes he could be here," she'd tell the kids, "but what he's doing is important. I'm so proud of him for how hard he works for us."

Neglect in one area often signals neglect in others. Not only was I underserving my family, I was underserving my health in those days too. I thought I could get along just fine eating junk and indefinitely postponing exercise.

But now, after working seventy to eighty hours a week, traveling countless hours through soulless airports, and missing far too many family events, the payoff was in hand. The massive bonus check in my pocket was proof it was all worthwhile. As I double-checked the number, all the zeroes before the period felt like validation.

When I finally arrived home, I was grinning from ear to ear. I had bagged the big one. Against all my expectations, however, Gail was . . . subdued.

"Babe," she finally said, "I really want to be excited for you, but we need to talk." Uh-oh. No high fives? No "Let's pop the champagne"? She led me into the den. As we sat down, I noticed her lip was quivering. She composed herself.

"You know, Michael, I love you," she said. "I'm so proud of you. I appreciate all that you're doing to support this family. But I gotta be honest. . . . You are never home. Your five daughters need you. Even when you are home, you're not really here. You're somewhere else." She paused, tearing up as she weighed her words. "Honestly, I feel like a single mom."

The Hustle Fallacy and the Ambition Brake

We all begin our professional lives, switch jobs, and take promotions with good intentions. No one starts by thinking, "The choices I make today will alienate my spouse and cause my children to hate me," or "The patterns I set now will lead to exhaustion and burnout," or "It's time to start trading my health for wealth."

Instead, we picture the financial, emotional, and social benefits that come from meaningful work. Our options are open, our future bright.

THE HUSTLE FALLACY

THE AMBITION BRAKE

But as stress and strains intensify at work, as they invariably do, many of us fall for the Hustle Fallacy. We think if we just crank a little harder, we can push past all the pressure. The demands keep mounting, and we try running faster still. We hope to catch up—maybe even get ahead—if we just work smarter and master personal productivity. But no matter what we do, the obligations outpace our hustle.

We work longer and sleep shorter; fix problems at the office while creating new ones at home; attend more meetings and skip more meals, games, and nights with friends; plan bigger projects and lead smaller lives. We assume we'll eventually be free to pause, relax, and give attention to our health and relationships. But before long, *eventually* becomes another way of saying *never*. Our life becomes what researcher Ann Burnett calls an "everydayathon."[2]

Presented this unattractive picture, some people opt for a completely different reality. They refuse to shortchange health or relationships and intentionally throttle back their career. Instead of hustling harder, they pump the Ambition Brake.

But this choice has trade-offs of its own. Applying the Ambition Brake might secure our health and family, but we end up with unused potential, reduced income, and other losses. Stress and crazy hours no longer crush our health or personal life, but unfulfilled professional dreams and ambitions could just as well crush our souls. And that's where my (Megan's) story comes in.

The Impossible Choice

As you might guess from my name, I'm Michael's daughter. I'm also the chief executive officer at Michael Hyatt & Co. Before taking that role, I served as chief operating officer for several years. But filling those roles almost didn't happen.

When my husband, Joel, and I got married, I was running communications at New Hope Academy, a nonprofit private school with a mission of racial reconciliation in Franklin, Tennessee. He was a vice president at Thomas Nelson.

After a couple years together, we decided to adopt two young boys from Uganda. They were only toddlers, but both had already experienced a lot of trauma. Still, we figured we were up to the challenge. We had Jesus, Target, and Whole Foods. That and a little love can solve anything, right?

We were in over our heads from the start. Shortly after we got home, I quit my job to care for our boys full-time.

But therapies and specialists don't come cheap. We couldn't afford the help we needed on Joel's salary alone. I had to find a part-time position somewhere.

Around that time, my dad launched Michael Hyatt & Co. Pretty soon he needed a part-time manager, and we figured I could do the job in about ten hours a week. Given our situation, that seemed like the perfect fit; so, I took the role.

We were off like a rocket. As the business raced ahead, my ten hours became twenty, and then thirty, and then forty. The scope of my role and size of my salary grew along with the hours. In fact, two years in, my earning potential exceeded Joel's. He quit Nelson and began freelancing, holding things together at home, while I pursued this rapidly scaling opportunity. That's when I faced an impossible choice.

Eventually, my dad and I realized we needed more than a manager. We needed a chief operating officer. We both knew I'd be great for the role. But I also realized it would be more demanding than anything I'd done before, and that presented a dilemma.

I could become the COO or successfully raise my kids. That's how it felt—an *or*, not an *and*. I could achieve my potential as an executive, but my children would suffer. Alternatively, I could turn my attentions home, but I'd have to take a back seat in the company I helped build. I could win at work, or I could succeed at life, but it seemed as though I couldn't do both.

A Better Solution

That's exactly how it felt to me (Michael) as I sat with Gail in the den all those years ago. I was winning at work. I was meeting and beating my numbers. I was leading my team. I couldn't let them down. They expected and deserved to go on to better, higher accomplishments. My boss did too. He was literally banking on it.

Of course, Gail and the girls also needed me. And I knew winning at life included additional areas worth my attention: health, friendships, hobbies, and all the pursuits and pastimes that make a well-rounded person. The choice couldn't be so binary as hustling or braking. There had to be a better solution.

When facing such an impossible choice, it's wise to look for a third option. The confrontation in the den wasn't the first time workaholism had caused problems in my marriage; I'll share another in the next chapter. But Gail's tearful protest was the most sobering to date. I had to find an answer.

I started to ask myself: Was there another way? One that wouldn't cost me my career or my family? One that didn't leave me with a lifetime of burnt bridges, failed health, financial disaster, and family regrets? What if I could win at work *and* succeed at life? It took several years of research, experimentation, and self-discovery, but I'm happy to report I found that elusive third option. We call it the Double Win. It's what my company is all about today. It's what this book is about now.

> **When facing an impossible choice, it's wise to look for a third option.**

We don't alter our trajectory by running faster or slower. As Andy Stanley says, "Direction, not intention, leads to destination."[3] We must imagine a different destination and then change our course to get there.

The Double Win sees work and life in partnership, not opposition.

Thankfully, around the same time I (Megan) contemplated the COO offer, I attended a conference where one of the speakers, a CEO of a very successful business and mother of several children, helped paint a different picture for me. She said, "There is nothing in my business so important that can't be handled between the hours of 8:30 a.m. and 3:30 p.m., so that I can be home with my kids without compromising my business results."

That was the first time I'd heard that perspective from a female executive. Her observation opened up a new sense of possibility. I didn't have to work fifty-plus hours a week and ignore my kids. Here was my third way.

I told my dad that I could take the job on one condition: I had to unplug from work and leave every day at 3:00 p.m. to pick up our kids from school. I wanted to be the one greeting them, fully focused on their day without the distractions of email, texting about business, or getting tied up on the phone. He agreed, I took the job, and I've been working some version of that schedule ever since.

My story is an example of the Double Win, which sees work and life in partnership, not opposition. They complement and fuel each other. Winning at work gives us the confidence, joy, and financial support necessary to support our personal priorities. Succeeding at life fosters a clear mind, creativity, and a rested body so we can focus on the work that matters most.

This is not an abstract hope. It's a concrete, daily reality. We live it. Our employees live it. Our coaching clients live it. And it's a real possibility for you as well. But there's an obstacle.

The Cult of Overwork

For most of us, our sense of what's possible is shaped by the cult of overwork. It's a widespread belief, one endemic to major corporations and small businesses alike. And it holds vast numbers of workers in its sway. Knowingly or not, to one degree or another, millions of us have accepted the idea that

- ► work provides the primary orientation for life;
- ► constraints stifle productivity;
- ► work-life balance is a myth;
- ► a person should always be busy; and
- ► rest wastes time that could otherwise go to work.

We may never consciously verbalize these ideas, and many of us would deny them when they're stated so clearly. But they hover in the background, nonetheless, quietly informing our thoughts and actions.

The impact of this belief system on our lives is staggering. Consider health. Eight in ten workers in the US suffer from on-the-job stress.[4] When we're under pressure, we tend to abandon healthy self-care habits, which amplifies the problem.[5] People who clock in excess of 55 hours each week raise their chance of heart attack by 13 percent and stroke by 33 percent, compared to those who work only 35 to 40 hours.[6] That's to say nothing of tension headaches, digestive troubles, higher blood pressure and cholesterol, decreased libido, and elevated levels of epinephrine and cortisol—all of which overworking contributes to.

What about relationships? Three-quarters of US professionals say stress undermines their personal connections.[7]

Entrepreneurs seem to suffer considerably higher divorce rates than others.[8] Same with CEOs.

These high-pressure jobs would be enough to strain any relationship, but long hours and singular attention to work drive marital breakdown. "The No. 1 reason why CEO marriages fail is lack of time for family," according to a story by CNN. "CEOs are almost always at work and when they're not, they're thinking about work." Said an attorney quoted in the story, "You end up with these fractured relationships where the husband and wife are almost living two separate lives."[9]

Overwork also damages job satisfaction, productivity, and more. A recent study by the Yale Center for Emotional Intelligence examined engagement and burnout in over a thousand US employees. Twenty percent of employees reported both high engagement *and* high burnout. They were passionate about their work, but they were suffering from it too.[10]

Constant stress and anxiety compromise our ability to think clearly and make good decisions. Our judgment goes out the window, and we make more mistakes than usual.[11] Not only does this produce diminished performance, but it works like a negative feedback loop. The cult of overwork is a self-reinforcing belief system. When overworked, we tend to think the answer is more work! It's a classic example of what economist Bryan Caplan calls an "idea trap."[12]

Good ideas tend to produce good outcomes, and good outcomes reinforce good ideas. But the reverse, as Caplan explains, is also true. Bad ideas tend to produce bad outcomes and reinforce bad ideas. "Once you fall into this trap," he says, "all it often takes is common sense to get out. But when people are desperate, common sense gets even less common than usual."[13]

Breaking free from the cult of overwork requires interrupting the negative feedback loop with new and better ideas. That's why we wrote *Win at Work and Succeed at Life*. We want to offer our fellow high achievers some of that hard-to-come-by common sense. In the pages ahead, we present not only a rejection of the cult of overwork but also a proven pathway you can follow to experience the Double Win for yourself. Let's talk about how.

Five Principles of the Double Win

High achievers feel compelled to overwork for a variety of reasons—some good, some bad, some inherent to the very nature of work itself. We'll spend time looking at those in the next chapter.

Then we will offer our counterproposal to the cult of overwork: the five principles of the Double Win. Here's an overview of each.

1. Work is only one of many ways to orient your life. There are several domains beside work. But family, friends, community, physical and emotional health, and all the rest are easily marginalized while pursuing career ambitions. The cult of overwork obscures the fact that success is only sustainable when most of these domains thrive together—which is a challenge.

Technology encourages work to backflow into our nights and weekends. And that eclipses other life-enhancing pursuits, which undercuts both our personal and professional lives. A culture that encourages employees to work all hours will damage the support structures that make those employees good at their jobs in the first place.

Life is multidimensional, and success is too. We bet you came to this book because you believe that to be true but haven't had the right tools to protect these other domains. We'll talk about how to do that as we go.

> **Life is multidimensional, and success is too.**

2. Constraints foster productivity, creativity, and freedom. Early in our careers, neither of us were taught to appreciate the power of constraints. But we all have a finite amount of time, money, energy, mental bandwidth, and creative capacity. Since we can't do everything, constraints force us to make choices. We have to decide where and how to best spend our time, money, and so on.

When working within the constraint, we experience tremendous gains. Not only does our productivity improve, but so does our capacity for fresh thinking. We're also free to engage our whole life, not merely the parts tied to our laptop or smartphone. Ironically, it's when we refuse to acknowledge life's natural constraints that they get the better of us. If, on the other hand, we embrace constraints, we can turn them into aids to achievement.

3. Work-life balance is truly possible. Many think achieving work-life balance is a myth because they assume balance is an attempt at some sort of Zen-like state of equilibrium when everything is in perfect proportion, perfect alignment. Once achieved, you're set for all time. Since that's impossible, they believe balance is likewise impossible. But that's not reality—nor is that what we're advocating.

Work-life balance is dynamic, not static. Consider the gymnast walking across a balance beam, or an acrobat walking the tightrope, constantly adjusting. Balance requires us to anticipate and deal with variables. It also requires us to weigh the different domains of life intentionally and with a view toward seeing they all get the attention they require. It's not about the perfect distribution of our efforts and interests, time and talents, or anything so precise. It's about not dropping the ball because we took our eye off it and forgot to check back.

Given cultural and workplace pressures, this is especially burdensome on professional women. We'll explore why and what can be done about that as well.

4. There's incredible power in nonachievement. High achievers struggle to hear this, but many of the most enriching, restorative activities in our lives are ends in themselves: hobbies, art, child-rearing, friendships, music, wine, crafts, games, and more.

This is difficult to embrace because high achievers want to measure everything. It's got to count or it doesn't matter. We're hardwired to pursue the all-important return on investment. But not everything is a goal. Not everything has an ROI outcome to measure—at least not in the short term.

Even more problematic is wrongly believing that achievement is always good, and nonachievement is pointless. As we'll see, it pays major dividends.

5. Rest is the foundation of meaningful, productive work. The cult of overwork devalues rest. Sleep is of no commercial

THE CULT OF OVERWORK	DOUBLE WIN PRINCIPLES
• Work is the primary orientation for life	• Work is one of many ways to orient your life
• Constraints stifle productivity	• Constraints foster productivity, creativity, and freedom
• Work-life balance is a myth	• Work-life balance is truly possible
• A person should always be busy	• There's incredible power in nonachievement
• Rest diverts time away from more work	• Rest is the foundation for meaningful, productive work

value, right? In fact, some regard it as the enemy. If we're not careful, we can view rest as a necessary evil, a biological need we begrudgingly endure to keep working and consuming.

Never mind the overwhelming body of evidence showing that sleep rejuvenates our mind and body, keeps us sharp, and powers performance. Sleep is not only the secret weapon of enhanced productivity, it's also the foundation for it.

When we undervalue sleep, we also fail to understand the negative consequences when we and our team are sleep deprived. We'll discover that rest is an active skill, and we'll gain a fresh appreciation for deliberate rest as a tool to stimulate and sustain creativity in work and life.

The Double Win Decision

We've both made a lot of sacrifices for our careers over the years. We're convinced the trade-off wasn't worth it—not only in terms of what it cost our personal lives but also what it cost our professional performance. What we missed for years, and what you might be missing right now, is that these aims can be achieved only in tandem. If we try advancing one at the expense of the other, we eventually fail at both.

That's why we've paired each of these principles with a practice to help you implement the principle and escape the cult of overwork. As you begin practicing these principles, we're confident you'll see your relationships, health, and well-being improve, along with your job satisfaction and performance. In fact, you'll be more productive, creative, and resourceful than ever.

During the last eight years, our team at Michael Hyatt & Co. has coached thousands of business owners, executives, and nonprofit leaders like you who find themselves facing the impossible choice. And, like us, they don't want to choose winning at work over being successful in life, or vice versa. Instead, they've committed to the Double Win and reaped the benefits.

Time and again we've seen leaders multiply their revenue *and* slash their hours. We've seen them achieve unprecedented success in their career *and* in their personal life. We've watched our coaching clients become more productive while at work *and* fully present when at home. They just needed a new approach. Maybe you're in the same boat.

We're grateful that a number of our clients have given us permission to share their stories with you in this book. As

you'll see from their accounts, the Double Win yields amazing returns.

It's never too late to steer the ship another direction. Imagine what could happen if you or your company were operating at full capacity instead of the mirage of it? An over-busy
life is not an economic necessity; it's a failure of imagination.

If you're all in on the Hustle Fallacy, or assume the only
alternative is to pump the Ambition Brake, we want you to
imagine something different: Picture what your life would
be like if you really had time for your career and your relationships and the time to take care of yourself. Does that
sound appealing, like something you'd like to experience for
yourself? If so, let's get started.

2

THE CULT OF OVERWORK

Work gives man nobility—and turns him into an animal.

ITALIAN PROVERB[1]

As a serial entrepreneur, Kyle has started multiple businesses, failed at some, sold some, and owns several others. Along the way, he worked for a large legal services company valued at $45 million with offices in Minneapolis, New York City, West Palm Beach, and San Francisco. He led a team of 365 people in operations, technology, and innovation. Kyle helped grow the business to $100 million and then the owners sold it to a private equity firm.

In order to reach that level of success, he admits he was "fully consumed and focused on work." Not only had he compromised his family life, but with 50 percent of his time spent on the road, he wasn't taking care of himself.

Perpetually exhausted and mentally depleted, Kyle was running on fumes. But he was driven. Expectations at work were high. And he wanted to impress his dad, someone who traveled 60 to 70 percent of the time when Kyle was young. But he couldn't keep up his pace forever. The bill for his neglected health eventually came due.

Kyle and several colleagues were dining at an upscale seafood and steak house in West Palm Beach, Florida. They were busy working on a large project. As dinner came to a close, Kyle grew dizzy. He swooned as he stood from the table, steadied himself, but still struggled. "As we moved down the hallway to the front door, I fell over and collapsed on the floor."

His coworkers picked him up, helped him to the car, and brought him back to the hotel room. The ride did nothing for Kyle's condition. In fact, he looked so bad they promised to touch base later in the evening to make sure he was all right. He wasn't. When their call came, Kyle was out cold.

Alarmed by his lack of response, his coworkers convinced the hotel manager to break into his room. "They found me passed out in a pool of blood on the bathroom floor," Kyle said. "I was rushed to the emergency room and placed in an MRI machine." That's when his breathing stopped. "I couldn't inhale or exhale," he said. "The last thing I remember was a doctor jumping up over me, grabbing me by the face, and saying, 'Kyle, you're going to be all right. Hang in there.'"

Three days later Kyle came to in the intensive care unit. He said he's always had strong faith, but this moment was a "come to Jesus" like none other. "I admitted the way I had been living wasn't right," he said. "I wasn't enjoying the insane pace. I was out of balance. I had put myself at risk of dying. And I had the gift of a second chance to make things right.'"

Kyle had been pushing himself so hard he had walking pneumonia. He'd been on antibiotics, but doctors said his immune system was diminished. When he ate lobster that fateful night, the dish contained bacteria that compromised his respiratory system and injured his stomach, causing him to bleed out.

With time in recovery, Kyle used his near-death experience for reflection: "I remember thinking, 'I don't want to miss everything. I want to be there for the important moments with my family.' You can't be there for everything, but there are some things that I just really want to be there for. The problem is, I'd get caught up in my work and the time just disappeared. The next thing I knew, three years were gone. I'd look back and think, 'Where did that time go? What did I spend my time on? And, were those things even important anymore?'"

A Future without Long Hours?

According to a study of how CEOs spend their time, the typical chief executive works about ten hours every weekday and puts in another eight most weekends. They also clock about two and a half hours per day most vacation days. In all, the study found CEOs averaged 62.5 hours a week on the job.[2] Of course, if you count the hours spent noodling on their businesses and distracted by concerns in their off hours, it's far more.

Modern technology has made overwork the norm. Research by the Korea Labor Institute found smart devices add more than eleven hours to the workweek, especially after the close of business.[3] Another study of executives, managers, and professionals found smartphones stretch the workweek to more than seventy hours for most.[4]

This doesn't mean professionals are deep in focused work for all those hours. But it usually means they are at least monitoring work, if not actively thumbing, swiping, and dictating their way through emails, messages, reports, as-signments, and everything else that piles up while stuck in meetings most of the official workday. Plenty of that happens too. And seventy hours might be undercounting.

Modern technology has made overwork the norm.

One unpublished Harvard Business School study found professionals either worked or monitored work more than eighty hours a week.[5] Don't forget, there are only 168 hours in a week. These kinds of hours can't help but edge out family, friends, rest, leisure, and even the basic business and regular errands of life.

According to pundits and theorists in the last century, none of this should be happening. Technology was supposed to free us from overwork, not saddle us with more. They predicted automation would provide us gobs of free time. In 1930, for instance, economist John Maynard Keynes said we'd only need to work fifteen hours a week. "Three hours a day is quite enough to satisfy the old Adam in most of us," he said.[6]

In 1932 philosopher Bertrand Russell said, "Modern technic has made it possible to diminish enormously the amount of labor necessary to produce the necessaries of life for everyone." He figured people could get by on just four

What they thought we'd be doing with modern technology

What we're actually doing with modern technology

hours of work a day. Russell had been saying so for almost a decade by then.[7] Many had.

Starting in the 1910s, a number of writers and commentators began speculating people would need to work no more than six, four, three, even as little as two hours a day. The only problem imagined was how to use the leftover hours. "The job which supports you will become a rather insignificant chore, and the hobby and the avocation will absorb most of your energies," said Clifford Furnas, a professor of chemical engineering, in 1932. "What to do? How to stay out of trouble?"[8]

This sort of thinking survived World War II and well beyond. *The Jetsons* cartoon, which premiered in 1962, imagined work reduced to pressing buttons a few times each day. When George Jetson wakes from a nightmare after working "two full hours," his wife, Jane, says his boss is running a sweatshop.[9]

The writers for the show were just playing with the prevailing assumptions about work in the future. "By 2000," *Time* predicted in 1966, "the machines will be producing so much that everyone in the US will, in effect, be independently wealthy."[10]

Of course, the prophets were wrong, at least partly. Twelve-to-fifteen-hour days used to be the norm for manual laborers. It's true that hours have decreased for most workers in those sorts of jobs. But that's not true for knowledge workers, executives, managers, creatives, and other professionals. Why is that?

Driven to Succeed

During my senior year at Baylor University, I (Michael) started my publishing career at Word Publishing in Waco, Texas. I landed a full-time job as the marketing director, and I was elated. At the time, Word was the worldwide leader in faith-based books, publishing bestselling authors such as Billy Graham.[11]

One small problem: I got the job because I was a better salesman than marketer. In fact, I had no real marketing experience. But there I was, suddenly responsible for all the advertising, merchandising, in-store promotion, and public relations for a major publisher—plus managing a staff.

Since I was underqualified, I was scared to death I'd be found out. I envisioned the head of HR knocking on my door. "Michael," he'd say, "the jig's up. We now realize you don't have an ounce of experience. Since you don't have a clue what you're doing, you have ten minutes to pack your bags." That fear drove me to prove I could do the job better than anyone else.

I also had an inherent, insatiable drive to achieve. My top strength, according to my StrengthsFinders profile, is *achiever*. I loved climbing the ladder. I loved succeeding. I loved going from one level to the next. I was constantly trying to beat last month's numbers. That translated into long hours.

In those early years, I arrived at the office at 5:00 a.m. and I wouldn't leave until 6:00 p.m. I even felt a little guilty for leaving so early. I'd usually be at my desk during lunch, so I typically logged thirteen hours a day. That's not counting drive time. Far too often, I'd leave the office late or I'd go home, wolf down a quick dinner with the family, and then park myself in the recliner, whip out my briefcase, and keep working. I usually went into the office on Saturday too.

I was working between seventy and eighty hours a week, sometimes more. But I eventually got used to the grueling pace. Or, at least, I became numb to it. My boss loved it. He praised my work ethic. He gave me the raise I needed, and I was soon promoted. Of course, the promotion led to additional responsibilities, which amped the pressure and upped my hours.

While I was driven to succeed and enjoying the pay and perks of my position, Gail was flying solo, patiently running the household. We had two small children at the time, and she really needed relief. She wanted us to be more than two ships passing in the night. She wanted to linger over dinner, to sit and talk about the day, maybe take an evening walk to process life as a couple.

With each passing month, we found ourselves becoming increasingly short, snippy, and testy with each other. One night things came to a head. "You know what?" I erupted. "I think this is really your problem. You're the one who's broken."

I'm wincing right now just remembering it. But I wasn't done. "You definitely need to go see a counselor to get your issues worked out," I said and added, "I'll pay for it." I sent my wife to a counselor while I kept working eighty hours a week. I was the one who needed my head examined!

After a few weeks with her therapist, Dr. P, Gail returned one night and said he wanted to see me at her next appointment. "This is something you all need to square away," I said, indignant. "I'm just a bystander here."

I wondered if they could record the sessions so I could listen to the cassettes on my commute. "I don't have the time for this. You know the crazy hours I'm putting in, right? I'm juggling everything to succeed at work for *us*." That's what every workaholic says. He's doing it for somebody else.

"I understand," Gail said, undaunted. "But he's really insistent. He doesn't think we can resolve this issue unless you're willing to come in. There are no recordings—it just doesn't work that way."

I finally relented. When the fateful day came for my first session, I drove directly to the counselor's office after work. Gail was already there. After some initial pleasantries, Dr. P asked me to tell him a little bit about my background. The more I talked, the more comfortable I felt. It wasn't as bad as I'd imagined. I should have known.

"Michael," Dr. P finally asked, "why do you think you're so driven?"

I didn't see that coming. It cut right to the core in a blink. It dawned on me I had abandoned Gail in the pursuit of my own ambition. I started to cry. I might have fooled her, but I didn't fool Dr. P. The issues in our marriage were not Gail's issues; they were mine.

The question hung there in the air. Why was I so driven? I knew my fear of failure was an initial factor. But there had to be more to it. I wasn't necessarily pursuing wealth. True, I seriously underestimated how expensive kids would be. Every time I turned around, Gail legitimately needed more money. I found myself constantly doubling down and working harder to keep one step ahead of the alligators. But isn't that the drill for most Americans? The answer was deeper still.

I returned to Dr. P's office for several weeks. In that time, I learned the problem had roots in my teen years. It's too challenging to recount the story in full, but suffice it to say I felt a profound sense of disappointment, even betrayal, from a person very close to me. In response, somewhere deep inside my heart, I made a silent vow: I was going to make something different, something better of myself. It became the driving force of my life.

That vow coded a new command in my operating system. It ran silently in the background, so unobtrusively I didn't even notice it most of the time, but it shaped how I thought about my presence and performance in all sorts of situations—especially work.

Thanks to Gail and Dr. P, I realized I could edit the code. My reactive commitment as a teen was not serving me any longer. I didn't have to compensate for what I endured as a youth by being a workaholic as an adult. I used to wear overwork as a badge. Now I recognize it was pathological.

I wish I could say those sessions with Dr. P were all it took to shake me free for good from the cult of overwork. Unfortunately, it took several years to finally break loose. Despite what the futurists and prophets like Keynes envisioned, overwork seems a constant temptation for many of us today. Why is that?

Why We Overwork

According to our experience and research, the reasons for overwork are many. Some are even inherent to work itself. So avoiding the slippery slope can be trickier than you might think. The following reasons are not exhaustive, but they do provide a good sense of the challenge we face.

Work is—can you believe it?—fun! After describing a work schedule that starts at half past five in the morning, Ryan Avent, a senior editor for the *Economist*, explains how he shuttles between home and the office, making time for his kids at the top and bottom of the day, but otherwise handling the tasks of his trade: writing, editing, and reading. "I work hard, doggedly, almost relentlessly," he says. "The joke, which I only now get, is that work is fun."[12]

Overwork
seems a constant
temptation
for many of us
today.
Why is that?

WHY WE OVERWORK

- Work is—can you believe it?—fun!
- Personal growth and identity
- The experience of flow
- Definable wins
- Status and value signaling
- Sky-high expectations
- The treadmill effect

We get it. We love the work we do. Most executives, entrepreneurs, and professionals we know and coach love their work too. That's something the futurists hadn't counted on—people would (and do) enjoy working!

Avent admits that many jobs are "grueling and thankless." But when it comes to knowledge work, he notes, much of the true drudgery has been eliminated, automated, or outsourced. As a result, he says, "my work—the work we lucky few well-paid professionals do every day, as we cooperate with talented people while solving complex, interesting problems—is fun. And I find that I can devote surprising quantities of time to it."[13]

He admits that such a life precludes more than the bare minimum time for family, hobbies, leisure, and so on. And from this one snapshot, it sounds as if he's handling the trade-off well. Of course, as we've seen and will see, that's not the case for many who work these sorts of hours.

The pleasures of work should not be discounted. Even if we dislike the pressures and particulars of a given task, we can love and value how solving a problem, hitting a deadline, closing a project, delivering a report, and shipping a product make us feel.

"Top professionals are the master craftsmen of the age," says Avent. "We design, fashion, smooth and improve, filing the rough edges and polishing the words, the numbers, the code or whatever is our chosen material. At the end of the day we can sit back and admire our work—the completed article, the sealed deal, the functioning app—in the way that artisans once did."[14]

Personal growth and identity. Keynes and others also underestimated the psychological satisfaction and growth found in tackling difficult problems individually or with our teammates. "Keynes," says Columbia University professor Edmund Phelps, "conveyed no sense of the role of innovation [creative problem-solving] in imparting excitement and personal development to business careers."[15]

We fool ourselves if we think work is primarily about mere subsistence and meeting our physical needs. It meets deeply felt psychological needs as well; we keep working as we hike up Maslow's hierarchy. Knowingly or not, most of us pursue our self-realization through our work. A career, as Phelps points out, has been the main context for this basic human need for some time now.

Philosopher Alain de Botton says work offers "alongside love . . . the principal source of life's meaning."[16] We can argue over whether that's good or bad, but it's pointless to debate the fact. Instead, it's best to realize, as with any good endeavor, it can become counterproductive and hurtful if we're not aware of the risks.

This possesses powerful pull. As work pressures mount, we respond by exercising our intellect, stretching our capabilities, testing our emotional stamina. While we expend extra energy on the job, possibly depriving our families and others of our energies, we feel rewarded for the effort. We feel alive to the accomplishment and made alive by it as well. Winning feels good. But if unaware, we can pursue those rewards to the detriment of other needs, which leads to all sorts of crises.

Winning feels good. But if unaware, we can pursue those rewards to the detriment of other needs, which leads to all sorts of crises.

The experience of flow. Avent relates the joy of accomplishment to the process itself, especially the state we enter when immersed in a challenge: *flow*. The term was coined by psychologist Mihaly Csikszentmihalyi. Experiences of flow, he explained, result from clear, challenging goals that require our best thinking and effort to accomplish. In states of flow, we are fully focused on the task at hand. We stop being self-conscious; time sails by. We are absorbed by the moment and what it requires of us.[17]

This is not true for all work, all the time. Sometimes we face projects that dwarf our skills. In those moments, we experience worry, anxiety, even dread. Conversely, we might have tasks that don't stretch us at all. In those cases, we experience boredom and apathy.[18] Either extreme can produce disengagement. Csikszentmihalyi pointed out that people surveyed while working express the desire to be someplace else more than when surveyed at any other time of the day.[19] That's especially true of male workers. The appeal of *Dilbert* comics and *The Office* sitcom speak to the experience. We've all banged our heads on pointless to-dos, baffling managers, and the rest. We laugh because it's true.

Despite these downsides, work does present frequent opportunity for experiences of flow. Studies by Csikszentmihalyi show that people experience flow more than half their working hours.[20] That's especially true for people who have been able to eliminate, automate, and delegate away the distractions and drudgery of their jobs. Entrepreneurs, executives, directors, creatives, and other professionals can submerge themselves for long periods of time in many rewarding aspects of building their business and serving their clients. They report being in flow about two-thirds of their time working.[21]

Definable wins. Flow is also possible with hobbies like cooking, playing music, or sports. But other domains of life outside work can sometimes feel immune from states of flow.[22] One condition for flow is feedback—performance indicators that let you know if you're doing well or not. We stay in flow as we process the feedback in the moment and improve our performance. Work not only contains clear goals that let us leverage our skills, but also includes feedback to assess our performance along the way. Not so in other areas of life, where we never really know if we're winning or not.

High achievers typically know what's required of them in the workplace. They understand what's expected and the benefits and perks that come along with meeting or exceeding those expectations. They can check things off their task list and move on to the next win. As such, they're comfortable in that environment.

That's not always the case at, say, home. Even when things are great, they rarely offer the same sorts of obvious wins that work does. That doesn't mean they aren't worthwhile, just that they require different sorts of engagement than does work. Relationships, parenting, home maintenance, cleaning, meal planning, laundry—these things never end. And some of them aren't remotely close to fun. We call work we loathe doing, but know we must, a *chore* for a reason.

Given these difficulties, it's easy to justify spending more time working, where the rewards are clear. Work can become an escape. Cartoonist Tim Kreider calls this "the busy trap," where workers become addicted to busyness and "dread what they might have to face in its absence."[23] The diapers, the dishes, the dusting, the dog all beckon, and such demands don't vanish by ignoring them. Often overworking means we have even less emotional energy to expend on them, inadvertently making them worse. There are some surprising differences with this challenge when it comes to gender that we'll explore in chapter 5.

Status and value signaling. "How are you doing?" someone asks. "Crazy busy," we respond. It's a way of signaling our status and worth—and possibly a faint effort at shilling for some sympathy.

"Stress makes Americans feel busy, important, and in demand," said *National Review* columnist Florence King, "and simultaneously deprived, ignored, and victimized.

Stress makes them feel interesting and complex instead of boring and simple, and carries an assumption of sensitivity not unlike the Old World assumption that aristocrats were high-strung. In short, stress has become a status symbol."[24]

King said this in 2001. A 2017 study by a trio of researchers confirms the judgment. They linked "humblebragging" about long hours on social media to perceptions about higher personal status. "Long hours of work and lack of leisure time lead to higher inferences in terms of human capital characteristics of the busy individual," the researchers found, "which in turn enhance the extent to which this individual is perceived as scarce and in demand, ultimately leading to positive status attributions."[25]

Scholar Ann Burnett noticed something similar. While studying thousands of holiday letters—the annual updates people send to family and friends on what's happening in their corner of the world—she saw busyness come up again and again. "We're busy, busy, busy," said one letter. "Our schedules have always been crazy, but now they're even crazier!" said another. Burnett noticed that people seemed to brag about how busy, stressed, and harried they were, as if racing through life was as laudable as Sally's home run and Timmy's college acceptance. "My God, people are *competing* about being busy," she said. "It's about showing status."[26]

A reputation for getting stuff done is objectively valuable, and maintaining an aura of busyness is one way to cultivate that reputation. It signals our value to peers and higher-ups. Who wouldn't want to be seen as in demand and essential—all the more if it positions you for advancement?

Sky-high expectations. Like all these reasons for overwork, this one becomes self-reinforcing. Being crazy busy is what's expected of both bosses and ourselves.

About fifteen years ago, I (Megan) had moved to a new city. I had taken a new, high-pressure sales job. It wasn't long before I started to experience stress-related symptoms and constant digestive discomfort. I was nauseated all the time. But rather than put constraints around my schedule, I doubled down on work. In spite of my physical condition, I had to go to work. I had to perform. I felt I had no choice; failure was not an option. I wanted to show my new boss he had made a great hire.

Before I grasped the severity of what was going on, which turned out to be a serious health problem caused by stress (I was later diagnosed with Crohn's disease), I remember going to work for several weeks with a bottle of Pepto-Bismol in my car's cupholder. To mitigate my pain, I literally drank Pepto-Bismol right from the bottle while driving down the road.

My situation went from bad to worse. I got deathly ill. I ended up having emergency surgeries during one of our family vacations. The physical toll of stress on my body took me out of life for about a year of intensive recovery because I was so sick. I had ignored those early physical symptoms, thinking I *had* to push through my workload.

Of course, it's not just individual workers who maintain these expectations. When you stick your toe in the corporate waters, you're stepping into existing business environments that can orient employee life around company goals at the expense of personal priorities. Bosses—often adherents to the cult of overwork themselves—want employees to match their enthusiasm for the job. They want them to be always on, always available.

Jack Welch, GE's iconic CEO, regularly worked Saturdays. "I thought these weekend hours were a blast," he recalled. "The idea just didn't dawn on me that anyone would want to be anywhere but at work."[27] Putting in hours on nights and weekends thus becomes part of the contract, even if never explicitly stated. If you want to advance, or keep your job, you have to give it your all. In the end, then, fear also becomes a powerful driver for overwork—not only fear that you might be found out as less than *qualified*, but also fear that you aren't up for the work *quantified*, especially as measured by the clock and calendar.

When we overwork, we may appear to be the star employee with an overnight success story. We may have convinced ourselves that at some point being so driven will pay off. As long as we can deliver results—or at least keep up appearances—it feels as if all is well. But the bridge is out, and we don't see trouble ahead.

The treadmill effect. Because work is directed toward completing goals, it's also in a way self-defeating. Every task has an *end* in both senses of the word—it has a purpose for which we labor and a point at which it's complete. As the Benedictine monk David Steindl-Rast asks, "How are you going to continue fixing your car once it's fixed?"[28]

When we derive so much fun, satisfaction, and significance from our work, finishing can be a mixed bag. For high achievers, completing a goal or project can be half thrill, half letdown. The source of our fun, satisfaction, and significance begins evaporating the moment we're done. "They are schemes for which success can only mean cessation," says philosopher Kieran Setiya.[29] As the thrill fades, we're left feeling the loss. If our primary source of fun, satisfaction, and significance is work, we might even feel empty or depressed by its absence. So we do the obvious—we find another goal and launch another project. In this way we end up on a treadmill, running away from disappointment and toward achievement, which, as we reach it, turns again to disappointment.[30]

Work contains its own justifications and so propels itself and us along, which is something of a blessing considering all the positives we gain from our labors. But if we're trying to extract something work can't provide, we'll end up frustrated and weary.

Escaping the Cult of Overwork

Again, these reasons aren't exhaustive. There are many personal, cultural, and systemic reasons people overwork. But it's important to note work itself contains aspects and features that induce us to overwork. It's no different than alcohol, food, exercise, or any other good thing people sometimes overdo. Unless we're alert to the risks, we can easily slip into patterns of overwork that might compromise our health, emotional well-being, families, social lives, and more.

Even when we know better, the draw is sometimes more than we're prepared to resist. NPR's David Kenstenbaum followed up with two family members of John Maynard Keynes, both of whom admit to regular overwork. Ironically, Keynes overworked himself. "His wife was very angry about it," one relative told Kenstenbaum. "She spent a lot of time trying to protect him from himself. . . . [I]n the end, he couldn't say no." He "died from working too hard," said the other. "You know, his heart ran out."[31]

Bertrand Russell noted the tendency back when he made his predictions. Instead of letting automation reduce workloads, he said, we've chosen to overwork. "In this we have been foolish, but there is no reason to go on being foolish forever."[32] We agree.

Kyle, our client we introduced at the start of this chapter, is a different man today. He joined our coaching program where he has learned another, better way. He told us that one of the benefits has been this simple change: "As a team leader, my team is no longer getting emails from me Sunday morning at 6:00 a.m. They don't feel obligated to respond on nights and weekends because I'm no longer reaching out to them. Both they and I have a stronger sense of peace within, a calmness that

> **Instead of letting automation reduce workloads, we've chosen to overwork.**

when we're not working, we don't have to be worried about work. And the team is loving our new norm."

People have greater control over their schedule than they think, though they may be unaware or in denial of the fact. Sometimes it can be easier to take on more rather than to have a tough conversation with a client or your boss. Beyond that, it can feel less threatening to overwork than to do an honest self-assessment and free ourselves. One great question is Dr. P's. Ask yourself,

▸ "Why am I so driven?"

And don't stop there. Ask,

- ▸ "Am I overworking to secure approval or affirmation?"
- ▸ "Am I working long hours to avoid my spouse or my kids?"
- ▸ "Why don't I delegate work that others can and should do?"
- ▸ "Am I secure in my position at work? Or am I fearful that without the long hours, I may be replaced by someone who appears to have more ambition?"

If you start asking these kinds of questions, others might surface as well. Your answers might surprise you. Sometimes we prefer living in self-denial, choosing to remain on the treadmill. The emotional payoff of overwork—fun, flow, significance—can divert us from the rest of our lives, which might be less fun and offer fewer opportunities for flow and personal significance. But whatever the reason you're driven to elevate work above the other domains of your life, it's never too late to restore your balance. Or find it for the very first time.

At the beginning of the book we outlined the false tenets of the cult of overwork. In this chapter we've encountered reasons it can be so powerful. Over the next five chapters, however, we'll explore the five principles of the Double Win and see how to break free. Let's look at the first principle now.

OUR MULTIFACETED LIVES

Work Is Only One of Many Ways
to Orient Your Life

I began to wonder why success . . . meant privileging
career achievement above all else.

ANNE-MARIE SLAUGHTER[1]

lon Musk is the CEO of automaker Tesla. He's also
the CEO of SpaceX, which seeks to colonize Mars.
Along with those multibillion-dollar companies, he
also runs a few significant side hustles.[2] As of this writing,
this forty-eight-year-old has a net worth of $41 billion and
he's the twenty-second-wealthiest person in the world.[3]

A visionary like Musk commands attention. After all,
we admire the scope of his ambition and his single-minded

dedication to making his dreams a reality. Many leaders, perhaps you, want to emulate him. But when we try, we come upon a serious problem.

Yes, Musk is a genius. He's also the honorary high priest of the cult of overwork. Musk advises entrepreneurs, for instance, to be "extremely tenacious and then just work like hell."[4] How much does he recommend? "Eighty-to-one-hundred-hour weeks every week." Sounds like hell. Is there a payoff?

Musk says we should do that because we'll accomplish three times what someone working forty hours a week can accomplish.[5] But productivity studies say just the opposite: hellish hours make us less productive. If anything, those extra hours only improve the odds our rocket will sputter midair when it comes to our health, relationships, and emotional well-being—maybe even explode.

When work is the primary orientation for life, the rest of life gets left behind. Musk's first wife, Justine, said, "Elon was obsessed with his work. When he was home, his mind was elsewhere." She felt ignored and neglected. "I longed for deep and heartfelt conversations, for intimacy and empathy," she said. "I sacrificed a normal family for his career."[6] They had five sons together, but their marriage lasted just eight years.

> **When work is the primary orientation for life, the rest of life gets left behind.**

Musk's sons also experience his inattention. "I don't see mine enough actually," Musk admitted, referring to his boys. "What I find is I'm able to be with them and still be on email. I can be with them and still be working at the same time."[7]

(Insert raised brow here.) So why does Musk feel the need to multitask when he's with his children rather than being fully present? "If I didn't," he says, "I wouldn't be able to get my job done."[8] That's what happens when work fills every corner of existence.

Musk gets very little sleep with the hours he keeps. At one point, while working out production kinks on the Model 3, he'd been sleeping so frequently on his couch at the Tesla factory—rather than his bed at home—his fans launched a campaign to buy him a more comfortable sofa.[9]

One lesson is clear from Musk's life: the Hustle Fallacy leads to self-neglect and minimal relational engagement. Musk must feel the void. After two failed marriages, he said in a moment of self-disclosure, "I would like to allocate more time to dating . . . I need to find a girlfriend . . . how much time does a woman want a week? Maybe ten hours? That's kind of the minimum?"[10] We're not relationship experts, but we doubt minimum viability is the right approach to lifelong romance.

Musk is a remarkable innovator. His vision and the products he creates are inspiring. Maybe his grueling methods will eventually get him the results he wants. The jury is still out on the long-term neglect of his health. But even if he's the rare exception who can happily neglect so much of his life, can his team? Or, more important for us right now, can you? Can your team?

We need to be constantly reminded that work is only one way to orient life. Life is multidimensional. Success can be sustained only when the majority of life's domains thrive together. Some people think the chance of explosive success in the work sphere is worth the wear and tear. Maybe in short spurts and sprints. As a lifestyle, it comes at a high price. You'll win at work and fail at life—which has blowback effects that cause your work to suffer too.

Driven to Success—or Excess?

When I (Megan) was ten years old, I really wanted to take up horseback riding. Since we didn't own a horse and couldn't afford such an expensive hobby, my parents struck a deal: If I could find someone who would swap stable care for riding privileges, Mom would drive me to the location. I was so motivated to ride, I took out a classified ad in the newspaper (remember those?), seeking someone who would exchange grooming their horse for riding privileges.

Turns out an older woman in the country had a beautiful white horse that she couldn't care for. She was happy to have me handle the horse's daily needs for a couple of years while I learned how to ride. By the time I reached my early teens, I was finally ready to exhibit. I had worked on perfecting the trot, canter, and gallop of my horse and couldn't wait to compete in a real horse show.

When the big day rolled around, Dad was too busy launching a new business to attend. That hurt. This was the thing I cared the most about and he wasn't there. Worse, my horse unexpectedly took off in the arena during the show and wouldn't stop until I got tossed. I hit the dirt and broke my tailbone. I remember driving home with my mom in the minivan in so much pain—and my dad wasn't there to support me when I needed his strength and words of comfort.

To his credit, Dad came to the really big stuff, like graduation. But candidly, I felt sad and even embarrassed that he wasn't at the normal stuff, such as the yearly parent-teacher meeting, because he delegated the "kid stuff" to Mom. From a kid's perspective, not being present doesn't work no matter how important your reason sounds.

My dad's choices during this season demonstrated his very narrow understanding of what showing up for the family meant. All we wanted was for him to be present. At meals. At bedtime. On vacation. And, while Dad felt compelled to pursue financial security, that wasn't the *most* important thing—at least not to us kids. We wanted him to spend time with us, being present in our world.

Because Dad was absent and Mom was so overwhelmed with five kids, I became a de facto third parent helping with the cleaning, taking care of my sisters, even potty training the youngest. Mom became overreliant on me to make up for what my dad should have done. In fact, at age fourteen, being super resourceful, I got a special "hardship" driver's license in Tennessee to help with grocery shopping. Can you imagine letting a fourteen-year-old drive?

As an adult with my own kids, I understand my parents' choices from a different angle. The financial pressure to provide for your family can be crushing. I understand that not just intellectually but experientially. Knowing that, however, I still don't give my dad a pass. Nor do I give myself a pass, or my husband. We have five kids, the same number my parents had. And what I know for sure is that the answer isn't to resolve the tension by opting out of more than half your life.

Work is only one of life's many domains. Depending on how you count them, there are at least nine more. When we coach our clients, we usually talk about ten domains in all:

- Spiritual
- Intellectual
- Emotional
- Physical
- Marital/Romantic

- Parental
- Social
- Vocational
- Avocational
- Financial

Every domain matters. Each impacts the others. Being stressed out at work impacts your relationships at home. If your health slips, that impacts your work. If you neglect your finances, you won't have a house to come home to. We need to be equally concerned about the world outside of work. The truth is, if you don't, you won't be winning at work for very long. Likewise, if you instinctively feel one or more of your life domains is out of sync, ignoring the issue will only make matters worse.

All Work and No Play

The easiest way to tell if work is your primary orientation is to ask how much attention you give the other domains. How much time do you spend each day, each week, on the spiritual, intellectual, and emotional? Do you make time for your health, your spouse, your kids, your friends? When is the last time you pursued a real hobby?

We've already seen the number of hours professionals are working. Given those time commitments, it stands to reason that many other life domains get shunted to the side. The Centers for Disease Control and Prevention, for instance, found less than a quarter of US adults get enough exercise.[11] Only about a quarter of workers use their annual vacation, and about 10 percent skip paid time off entirely.[12]

Even when we take time away from the office, we bring the office with us. A survey of a thousand American workers found more than half check their work email during family outings, while four in ten did so during dinner.[13] Two in three employees report working while on vacation.[14]

Interestingly, it's the professional class who tends to work the most hours. Keynes and the futurists were right about automation shrinking work hours. But the greatest reductions have been among service-sector and low-skilled workers. Meanwhile, professionals now work the same or more than they did in 1965.[15]

Economist Robert Frank recalls having dinner at the home of a billionaire, joined by a venture capitalist and tech engineer. "During the two hours I was at his house, he took six cellphone calls, sent 18 emails, and thought up two new business ideas," Frank said. "At the end of dinner he took his last sip of wine and said, 'It's so nice to be able to have a relaxing dinner at home.' I laughed. He didn't get the joke."[16]

Relaxing is an interesting word choice. Go back to the reasons for overworking in the prior chapter. Work is fun. It has definable wins. It's where we experience personal vitality and growth.

For high achievers who have tailored their jobs around their passions and proficiencies, work can be an extremely enjoyable, pleasant, comfortable environment. It's where some people feel most like themselves. But because it's so

There's a big difference between having **meaningful work** and having a **meaningful life.**

easy—at least by comparison to other domains—we can underattend the rest of our life. Work becomes the primary referent in our identity, almost like a religion.[17]

But there's a big difference between having meaningful work and having a meaningful life. "All work and no play," as the old saw goes, "makes Jack a dull boy." There's real wisdom there. If we don't occasionally stop to sharpen a blade, it gets dull and requires more effort to achieve the same result.

The same is true for us and our need for self-care and a more balanced lifestyle. Left unchecked, short-term wins at work often come at the expense of long-term life priorities. Sustainable success at work is dependent on the symbiotic integration with other life pursuits. But despite our best efforts, it's not easy.

Three Nonnegotiables

Some days it feels like our calendars own us instead of the other way around. How are we supposed to get it all done? After all, high achievers are in high demand and our workloads keep growing. We, in turn, tend to dip into time allocated for personal priorities, setting those aside for the sake of the work we have to do.

A primary reason we overwork is because we don't have clarity on what matters most. As a result, we shotgun everything on the horizon instead of maintaining focus on a few nonnegotiables—namely our self-care, relational priorities, and professional results. "Our dilemma goes deeper than shortage of time," says author Charles Hummel, "it is basically a problem of priorities."[18]

THREE NONNEGOTIABLES

1. Self-Care
2. Relational Priorities
3. Professional Results

So, how do we maintain focus on our nonnegotiables? By blocking out the necessary time on our calendars. This ensures we cover what matters even amid incessant demands and tempting propositions. If you don't, the urgent will swamp the important.

Think about your monthly budget. If you don't allocate the mortgage in advance, you can't pay it with leftovers. Too often that's exactly what we do with our time. Our most important priorities never make it onto our calendars; as a result, they get the leftovers and largely go unattended. But if time is money, as the saying goes, the answer lies in budgeting time for your nonnegotiables, same as the mortgage. There are three primary categories that need attention.

Self-care. Your health, your relationships, your children, your hobbies, your work—at the center of all of these is *you*. You're all you have to offer these various facets of your life. "You are a dimension of every problem or personal interaction you face," as historian Richard Brookhiser put it. "You are the tool that is never put back in the box."[19] If you're not nurturing yourself, if your self is not thriving, then the influence you bring to these other dimensions is going to be less than what it could be.

Oftentimes we view self-care as either a luxury or a selfish indulgence. Maybe you've said to yourself, "When my kids are older and sleeping through the night, I'll prioritize self-care," or "When that product launch is done, I'll have room for self-care," or "When the kids are finally out of the house, I'll have time for self-care."

Here's the problem. There's never a perfect time for selfcare. There are always other demands on our time. If we don't fight these intrusions, we end up sacrificing self-care as a matter of habit.

Self-care comprises activities that make for a meaningful life outside of work while contributing to greater performance at work. It refers to practices and habits that rejuvenate our bodies and minds: getting ample sleep, eating well, exercising regularly, connecting with the people we love, engaging in meaningful hobbies, and making time for personal reflection. "Rather than narrowly defining self-care as just physical health (which is an important piece of the equation)," says executive coach Amy Jen Su, "we need to pay attention to a wider set of criteria, including care of the mind, emotions, relationships, environment, time, and resources."[20]

The consequence of self-neglect is that our physical and mental well-being negatively affects our performance. We cannot lead ourselves or others well if we're exhausted or burned out and, in turn, we can't produce the results our clients, customers, bosses, or coworkers are counting on.

On the other hand, self-care has many benefits—not least of which is energy, a competitive edge, and endurance.

Most of us struggle to be consistent with this in part because we view self-care as just one more thing on our already overloaded to-do list. That's why we've found it beneficial to come back to the basics: Are you sleeping? Rest is the foundation of meaningful, productive work, as we'll explore more fully in chapter 7. Suffice it to say for now, there is no more essential self-care practice than getting adequate sleep, and yet sleep is usually the first thing we shortchange when we overwork.

Self-care has many benefits—not least of which is energy, a competitive edge, and endurance.

What about eating well? We're not talking about a diet here; we're talking about feeding your body so your brain can function and you can be present for the activities that matter most in your life. The brain makes up 2 percent of the body's weight but takes 20 percent of the body's energy to power it.[21] "Your brain requires a constant supply of fuel," says Eva Selhub of Harvard Medical School. "What you eat directly affects the structure and function of your brain and, ultimately, your mood."[22] If you're not eating well, you're not thinking well either.

Third, are you moving your body? Notice we didn't start with "exercising." That word can hang us up. Suddenly we're down the path of gym memberships and personal trainers when we just need to take a walk. If you've struggled with this, if you feel like you can never get consistent movement in your life, start by taking a stroll on your lunch break or after dinner. Include a friend if you can.

If you're an athlete and you love intense exercise or movement, go for it. But if this has been hard for you, lower the bar. Maybe just go out with your dog in the morning for fifteen or twenty minutes. Studies show a direct correlation between bodily movement and brain functioning. Even low-impact exercise nourishes your brain cells and promotes the growth of new ones.[23] When we exercise our legs, we are, as one study said, exercising our brain.[24]

Movement lowers our stress and anxiety levels while at the same time raising our sense of self-efficacy. In other words, it increases the belief that we can accomplish difficult tasks, which can, in turn, fuel greater performance at work and in other areas of our life. That might explain why it's even been linked to higher earnings. Researchers in Finland followed 5,000 male twins over the course of thirty years. They tracked which were sedentary and which were active, and they came to the conclusion that regular movement and exercise resulted in greater long-term earnings, as much as 14 and 17 percent higher.[25] Raising your heart rate might help raise your income.

What are your self-care nonnegotiables and where will you fit them in? Do yourself a favor. Block these on your calendar. They should get priority, not leftovers. As the writer David Whyte says, "To rest is not self-indulgent. To rest is to prepare to give the best of ourselves."[26] What's keeping you from making a commitment to self-care now?

Relational priorities. Just like self-care, we need to schedule our relational priorities. For me (Megan), this includes being present with my kids after school. As a working mom, this is quite the feat to make happen, but it's nonnegotiable. I want to have dinner at home with my family five nights a week.

The research on the effects of kids who grow up having regular family dinners is compelling. Writing in the *Washington Post*, Anne Fishel of the Family Dinner Project points to studies that credit family meals with reducing teen use of alcohol, tobacco, and drugs, along with lower incidence of eating disorders, suicidal thoughts, violence, trouble at school, and premature sexual activity.[27]

You can see why the simple act of eating together as a family ranks high on my priority list. Furthermore, I want to go on a regular date with my husband, Joel, each week. We also attend church on Sundays. Not very complicated, but those are the cornerstones of my relational nonnegotiables. I block them on my calendar. What gets scheduled is less likely to be unintentionally forgotten or squeezed out by something else.

Maybe for you it's blocking out your kid's athletic events or performances. Maybe it's a quarterly overnight getaway with your spouse. Joel and I have done that for a long time and love it. But if it didn't get on our calendar, there's no way we'd have a spur-of-the-moment getaway with a houseful of young children. We have to plan for it in advance if we want the win.

Maybe for you it's an annual fishing trip with some of your best friends from college, or a Christmas shopping trip in the city. Maybe it's weekly coffee or monthly lunch with friends. Maintaining these sorts of relationships can be a challenge for high achievers. And yet, good friends are essential to your personal growth and well-being. If it's a relational nonnegotiable, get it on your calendar.

A word of caution: If you don't have meaningful relationships apart from work, that's not too healthy. At the very least, it's not good risk management; if you change jobs, for instance, your social network will evaporate.

Fast-forward to the end of your life. What will you wish that you had done differently? Palliative care nurse Bronnie Ware recorded the regrets of her dying patients. Among the five most common? "I wish I hadn't worked so hard." Bronnie observes, "This came from every male patient that I nursed. They missed their children's youth and their partner's companionship. . . . All of the men I nursed deeply regretted spending so much of their lives on the treadmill of a work existence."[28]

Another of Bronnie's top five was relational regret. "I wish I had stayed in touch with my friends," she heard from many. "Many had become so caught up in their own lives that they had let golden friendship slip by over the years," she said.[29] If you want to avoid that regret, ask yourself, "What are my relational nonnegotiables?"

Professional results. This is the last in our list, but it's also essential. To succeed, we must drive results at work. That's true whether you're a business owner or an executive, an individual contributor in a larger team or a middle manager. This begins with clarity on the results you're responsible to produce. What do you deliver?

In my (Megan's) role as CEO of Michael Hyatt & Co., I'm responsible to deliver our annual budget, develop our executive team, and build the vision for the future. I keep these three professional outcomes in the forefront of my mind. I use them to inform and prioritize my decisions about how to spend my time. There are tons of worthy, though optional, requests or opportunities that hit my desk every day.

But by blocking my calendar with the necessary space to accomplish my "need to do" list, the optional things fall away.

For this level of clarity, you have to identify what drives the results you're responsible for and block time for those activities. For me, that's coaching my direct reports, brainstorming ways to optimize current initiatives, leading monthly executive financial reviews, and making final decisions on major initiatives. I can do this because I'm clear on where I add the most value.

This helps me know where to say yes and where to say no, not only now but also in the future. And that's important because, as leaders, we're always running both the business we have right now and the one we want to next year and the years thereafter.

Here are two questions to consider when thinking about building for the future: "What do I need to be planning or investing in today to produce results for tomorrow?" And "How can I take my ability to lead and drive results to the next level so that I can get us to the future I want?"

We overlook or postpone answering such questions because we feel as though we don't have time. We think maybe next year we'll work on envisioning the future. But kicking the can down the road means stagnating or declining revenues; when you have no new ideas, you can't drive growth. Just as bad, if you're not building yourself and your business for the future, you'll hold back your business and your team. Your star players might not stick around.

Think about the future results you want to create and ask yourself what your professional nonnegotiables might look like. For example, it could be making time for brainstorming new initiatives, or upgrading infrastructure for future scaling. Maybe for you as a leader it's quarterly coaching.

What are your professional nonnegotiables? After you've blocked them on your calendar, you may think, *Well, there's not a lot of time left.* That's to be expected. Your calendar has been trying to tell you that for years now. By blocking time, you can finally see what it's been saying: time is short. But time is also ample. And now you've accounted for what your nonnegotiables require. Nothing is missing except stuff that is, candidly, optional.

This Is Your Life

One of our coaching clients, Chris, was "always on," expected to return texts anytime day or night, or attend a fundraiser at the drop of a hat. But he wisely made a career change so he would have time for his marriage, to raise a family, and to invest in his health. Here's how he arrived at his decision to change.

Chris's first job out of college was in the political world, as the executive director of a large political action committee in Southern California. "Essentially we raised ungodly amounts of money for politicians to get elected," he says. He rubbed shoulders with bigwigs in and beyond the Golden State: congressmen, senators, governors, all the way up to the White House. "I was a young guy gaining a ton of responsibility and power."

Chris was personal friends with the mayor of one of the state's more prominent cities. The mayor was young and newly married with their first baby. "I walked alongside him during his reelection bid," he said. "I got to see firsthand how he was constantly connected to his BlackBerry. He *never* saw his family. From breakfast at 6:30 a.m. with constituents, sponsors, and fundraisers, to cocktail parties and dinners with high net-worth individuals—that was his life for about two years. He and his wife were nothing more than roommates."

The example proved beneficial for Chris. How? By demonstrating we can choose to do *anything* we want; we just can't accomplish *everything* we want. No one can orient their life so exclusively around work and maintain their health and relationships.

> **We can choose to do *anything* we want; we just can't accomplish *everything* we want.**

"Candidly, I couldn't fathom living like him," Chris confessed. "I'm thinking, 'You have a brand-new baby. Do you even get to hold your baby anymore?' He had a marriage by ring only, right? And yet, as I thought about this, *I* was becoming that same kind of guy." Chris realized he was slowly ceding his life to the cult of overwork, just like his friend.

"I was making great money," he said. "I had an amazing network of connections. I was called upon to have breakfast, lunch, and dinner with key leaders and donors. Most of my job was wining and dining them at their country clubs, at their second homes, asking for checks. Meanwhile, my wife, Alicia, and I started to become like ships passing in the night. I was sometimes up and out the door before she woke up, and returned after dark."

Chris was oriented totally toward work and just awakening to the fact he was leaving the rest of his life unattended at the very time other domains were rising in importance. He and Alicia were five years into their marriage and talking about having kids.

Driving one day, he began to think, *I'm not the husband I need to be and there's no way I'll be the dad that I could or should be.* Those thoughts ran through his head just as the Switchfoot song "This Is Your Life" came on the radio: "This is your life, are you who you want to be? . . . is it everything you've dreamed?" He had to pull over.

"I started weeping," he said. "I knew what I was doing and the person I was becoming wasn't who I was created to be. This wasn't the role I needed to play, both in the corporate world and in my home. Especially since I had always dreamed of being a great father." The moment was pivotal for him.

"Honey, I need to leave politics," he came home and told Alicia. He wasn't sure how she'd take the news. Leaving the only job he'd had would be disruptive. But Alicia understood the gravity of the situation.

She picked up a napkin from the kitchen table. "Okay," she said, "let's figure out how to make this happen." She started making a list: "What are we good at? What did we study? What are we gifted at? What are our interests?"

Through that back-of-the-napkin brainstorm, Chris and Alicia identified a new entrepreneurial venture, one that became their bread and butter. Using our productivity methods and tools, they designed a lifestyle enabling him to work from home with the margin and flexibility to be engaged with the family.

Rather than missing meals due to endless political fund-raising meetings, for instance, now Chris enjoys most weekly meals with his family. Chris has modeled a healthy work-life win that even his young daughter has noticed. "Daddy," she recently told him, "I hope my husband can stay home all the time like you do."

Chris couldn't be happier about his decision to make time for other important pursuits beyond work. In fact, he's mentoring his employees to understand that their sustainable success at work is dependent on the symbiotic integration with their life outside of the office. Here's what he tells them:

"I tell my company to get their work done when you need to get it done. But if your daughter has a school recital at 10:00 a.m. on a Wednesday morning, be there. If there's a day when you'd like to take your son to lunch at school, do that. We keep our workday flexible because, while I appreciate your great work, life happens with your spouse and your kids. Make sure that is given the proper place in your life."

In my life, achieving the Double Win would look like

Define Your Own Double Win

Elon Musk is a compelling figure, but only if you want one-sided success—and want to risk losing even that. We want to encourage you to imagine a different reality.

You don't have to live a life where you're overwhelmed, constantly stressed, frustrated, and creatively burned out. This new reality begins with imagining a different future outcome. For many leaders, they may have to suspend disbelief that nothing can ever be different. We coach tons of clients who wrongly believe they're doomed to that false reality.

Candidly, most of us put ourselves in a position of being the victim, as if this stress-producing lifestyle is being done *to* us rather than we're doing it to ourselves. In some respects, the culture reinforces the notion that we're powerless to do anything other than go with the flow.

When we think about the reasons we overwork, we tend to focus on the cultural and systemic reasons. By externalizing the reason, we can absolve ourselves of responsibility. It's entirely possible you work in an environment immune to good sense about overwork. If that's the case, you might want to consider changing jobs. But if you love your work, you must take responsibility for what you can change and change it. If you let it, the drift of the culture, like a riptide, will pull you in the opposite direction of the Double Win.

You have a choice. You can either live on purpose, according to the plan you've set. Or you can live by accident, reacting to the demands of others. The first approach is proactive; the second reactive. No, you can't plan for everything; things happen we can't anticipate. But it's a whole lot easier to accomplish what matters most when we're proactive, begin with the end in mind, and use our calendars to live the life we desire.

The process begins by admitting we're not Superman. We don't have a cape. We can't face insurmountable odds and accomplish *everything* that comes our way. Since it's impossible to do *everything*, we can't make *doing everything* our definition of success. It's important for us to stop and clarify the kind of success we're after.

A more realistic approach, then, is to define *winning* as achieving the things that matter most to me—at work and at home. We're talking about doing the things that drive results. Only you know what that means for you. That's the good news, because you get to define what success looks like for you.

Former Disney executive Anne Sweeney put it this way: "Define success on your own terms, achieve it by your own rules, and build a life you're proud to live." When you define the win at work, consider these questions:

- What's my unique contribution?
- What are the things that only I can do?
- Which of my activities drive the biggest results?
- Where do my skills and abilities best match my passions and interests?
- Where do I want to be in my career three years from now?

For me (Megan), I know I'm winning at work when we're meeting or exceeding our financial goals, when our leadership team is growing in their leadership and effectiveness, when I'm delegating at a high level and I'm very clear on where I add the most value, and when I'm proactively growing my own leadership and our vision for the future of our company. My win does *not* look like attending every meeting or making every decision. It's just impossible and certainly not desirable.

When you define the win at home, consider these starter questions:

- Where can I invest my time to make the people I love feel loved by me?
- How do I want to be remembered by the people who matter the most to me?
- What steps can I take to ensure proper self-care and good health?
- In what ways can I invest in my marriage to help it thrive?

For me, a win at home means being the one who opens the door for my kids at the end of the day when they're home after school. It means eating a home-cooked dinner around our table and practicing gratitude and connection. And it means spending time and having fun with Joel.

My win does not include travel soccer, being the Boy Scout den mother or president of the Parent Teacher Organization at school, or volunteering to be the Class Mom. Those commitments may be on your list. Nothing wrong with that. But I've decided those activities are not what *my* win looks like.

Each of us gets to decide which wins we're going to pursue and which ones we won't. Remember, we invest our limited time for maximum return on investment in the things that matter most to us—not to our neighbors or the broader culture.

One of the biggest obstacles to achieving the Double Win is the failure to remember that work is only one of many ways to orient our lives. Far too many people never stop to consider what they want to be true of their relationships, or their health, so they drift to a destination they wouldn't have chosen.

If you're unclear how you stand relative to life's other domains, consider using our free LifeScore Assessment tool. This resource provides a quick and easy snapshot of the relative health of each life domain and pinpoints areas where you might consider making some intentional improvements. You can find it online at WinAndSucceedBook.com/lifescore.

4

LIBERATION THROUGH LIMITS

——— PRINCIPLE 2 ———

Constraints Foster Productivity, Creativity, and Freedom

Irrespective of who invents and owns our job, we can still be the creator and owner of our work.

ROBERT KEEGAN[1]

Our client Tiffany runs an agricultural business in Florida with her brother, Paul, also a client. They raise hundreds of acres of sod along with organic produce. A few years ago, they bought the business from their dad, who started it in 1987. Tiffany began working for the company straight out of college about fifteen years ago. "When I graduated college, I worked my booty off," she said. "I thought there was a direct correlation with success in your business and number of hours worked."

Tiffany's assumption makes sense on the surface. The more you work, the greater your results. It sounds right. And business gurus proclaim it like Moses hiked down the mountain with it etched in stone.

We already heard from Elon Musk in the last chapter: "Work like hell . . . eighty-to-one-hundred-hour weeks every week." Investment guru Grant Cardone says instead of working the hours nine-to-five, entrepreneurs should work ninety-five hours—more than thirteen hours a day, every day of the week. And social media influencer Gary Vaynerchuk says entrepreneurs should put in eighteen-hour days to get their business off the ground.[2] But Tiffany found that math didn't work very well.

"Unless we were on vacation," she said, "maybe once a year, there was not a weekend that I didn't work. And also evenings. I was constantly going back to work, to the office, to the farm. I would always try to sneak away for a couple hours on the weekends or at night to get things done."

She did see some results from all those extra hours. Tiffany and Paul grew the business after they took it over. "You have your head down and you're just going, going, going." But the business didn't grow much or fast. And there was a cost, not only to her personal life, but to the business itself.

It turned out the correlation was false. "We did have some growth," she said, "but I was just working a lot and having those days where you get done and you don't really necessarily know exactly what you did, but you're tired."

Tiffany told herself it was temporary. But the marginal gains they were getting took everything she had, and there was no indication she'd be able to let up. In fact, according to popular guru math, she needed to invest even more time. Trouble was, she really didn't have any more to give. She knew something was wrong. She knew she needed a better equation.

Work Expands . . . and Contracts

Work is like water. It's life-giving. It also flows wherever it can unless otherwise constrained. We need hard edges to access its life-giving properties; think about what reservoirs and drinking glasses do for us. Without those hard edges, water can be destructive; think about a river overflowing its banks and flooding low-lying streets and homes.

Because of the reasons for overwork we covered in chapter 2, there's a tendency for work to overflow its banks and flood the other domains. Work often pushes itself into our personal and relational time. We work early in the morning before the workday rather than taking a walk or going to the gym. We stay too late at the office and miss dinner with the family. We use the weekends to try and catch up or get ahead on our assignments at the expense of other nonnegotiables, such as self-care and relational priorities.

Real or imagined, there's an expectation that we're connected 24/7 via email or phone. But responding to work-related business outside of office hours means we're no longer present for other meaningful domains. As a result, we bring something less than our best to both home and the office. By failing to guard our nonnegotiables, we're scattered and depleted.

We've all fallen into Tiffany's trap, thinking, *If I just work a little bit harder right now, we'll get the payoff, the rest, the family time, the me time—whatever—later.* But as we all discover sooner or later, there's really no end to working. It's easy to live in denial, thinking the extra hours will be temporary. But in the blink of an eye, three, five, and ten years slip by, and we're still overworking while our life spins off another direction.

The solution? Create hard edges around your workday, workweek, and weekend. You probably know Parkinson's Law: "Work expands so as to fill the time available for its completion."[3] Well, here's Hyatt's Corollary: "Work contracts to the time permitted."

According to the cult of overwork, constraints stifle productivity. But as we'll see, constraints actually foster productivity through creativity. That might sound counterintuitive on the face of it. But constraints at work liberate and empower us, allowing us to bring our best not only at home but also at work—especially at work.

Constraints foster productivity through creativity.

Just as we intentionally constrain water to better serve our needs, we must intentionally constrain our workday. When we employ constraints, we create the margin that frees us from overwork. We then become free to fully enjoy the work we have in the time we have, free from the "time creep" that happens when we permit work to fill evenings and weekends. We're free to invest in our health and other life domains. And just as important, we start to see real gains at work as well.

The inconvenient truth is that we don't have much say in the matter anyway. Constraints are real even if we pretend they're not.

The Reality of Constraints

We only have so much mental energy and physical stamina; eventually, we have to sleep, even if we're resentful of the fact. Time is similarly constrained. We only get 24 hours a day, 168 hours a week. Constraining our workday and work-week is about intentionally working within the constraints we already have to improve our experience, maximize results, and enjoy life more in the process.

We can't do everything. As Tiffany can attest, working harder or longer doesn't make you more productive. In fact, studies routinely show that productivity goes *down* after fifty hours per week. As Stanford researchers have documented, "Workers who put in 70 hours produce nothing more with those extra 20 hours. They're merely spinning their wheels, working longer hours but accomplishing less."[4]

Erin Reid, a professor at Boston University's Questrom School of Business, failed to uncover any evidence employees who worked eighty hours accomplished more than their colleagues who didn't. It turned out their bosses didn't either. "Managers could not tell the difference between employees who actually worked 80 hours a week and those who just pretended to," her research revealed.[5] That's mainly because there are no gains to notice beyond 50 hours of work. Net gains are nonexistent.

Instead, we're discovering nowadays that we must look on the other side of the forty-hour workweek divide for productivity gains. Some workers make their biggest contribution closer to the thirty-hour mark. Knowledge work, while seemingly less straining than physical labor, is seriously demanding. Knowledge workers are only good for about six hours a day. As writer Sara Robinson said after looking at the data, "You can stay longer if your boss asks; but after six hours, all he's really got left is a butt in a chair. Your brain has already clocked out and gone home."[6]

A study of Microsoft employees' workweeks confirms the point. While they clocked forty-five hours on the job, only twenty-eight were productive. That's just under six good hours a day.[7]

We've certainly felt the utter mental exhaustion that comes with this kind of work. We can grit it out and push to eight, nine, even ten hours. But we sense that our effectiveness declines as the hours increase. We can get frustrated over the fact. It's only a report, a spreadsheet, whatever. It's not that hard! Just knock it out. But we also know it's more than that.

When trying to understand what makes workers unhappy, Harvard professor Robert Keegan noticed the heavy intellectual and emotional participation needed of modern workers. Knowledge work requires us to essentially "*invent* or *own* our jobs," as he says.[8] There's the objective part of our job: explicit job descriptions, goals, projects, deadlines, and so on. But there's also the subjective part of our job: personal initiative, self-evaluation, and project analysis, not to mention the responsibility for results, expectations regarding personal growth and expertise, and other draws on our intellect, imagination, and emotional resources.[9]

Contemplating the demands of any particular job, we normally focus on the exterior, objective requirements. That part seems challenging but doable, even for long stretches of time. But the interior, subjective requirements are just as integral, even if they're invisible. And they all come with a cost. We can't keep that amount of intellectual and emotional effort going as long as we assume.

We have not only our own declining levels of effectiveness to factor but also the simple limits of available time. It's just math. There are 168 hours in a week. We're going to have to sleep for some of those hours, and we must take care of our physical needs as well: eating, bathing, and the other essentials. We can either resent that reality, or we can see these constraints as a gift. How so? Because they force us to clarify, prioritize, and be intentional about what we choose to do.

> **We have not only our own declining levels of effectiveness to factor but also the simple limits of available time.**

Constraints Enable Focus

For the longest time, one of the biggest challenges I (Michael) faced was that I had a borderless work environment. There were no boundaries whatsoever around my job. I didn't have a "quit time." Even if I did manage to get home for dinner at 6:00 p.m., I'd crack open the laptop and put in several more hours. On the weekends, like Tiffany, I'd sneak back to the office. That was before I embraced the constraint of time.

When I became the CEO of Thomas Nelson in 2005, it was the biggest job I'd ever had. We were a publicly held company, traded on the New York Stock Exchange. I had investors, a board, 650 employees, and thousands of customers to please. I quickly realized I could work all 168 hours in a week and still not get it all done.

Thankfully, I had a coach at the time who encouraged me to set three hard boundaries: don't work after 6:00 p.m.; don't work on the weekends; don't work on vacations. At first I only paid attention to the *don'ts*. It took a moment to understand how this affected what I *did*.

The constraints forced me to make efficient use of my time at work. Prior to that, I would often get distracted, especially in the afternoons. Then I'd think to myself, *If I don't get this done before I leave the office, I can do it at home after dinner.* Cue Parkinson: Work expands to fill the time allowed. But my self-imposed 6:00 p.m. curfew made this impossible. (That was the origin of Hyatt's Corollary.)

The constraint helped me stay focused and avoid pointless activity. I didn't have the luxury of getting distracted or wasting time on fake work. The constraint of time forced me to be selective and budget my work hours so I was free to focus on the other spheres of life while being more productive at the office.

We've experienced that as a company too. I (Megan) mentioned in chapter 1 that I've been working a six-hour day for years now. I'd been wondering for a while what would happen if we rolled that out across the board. Companies all over the world have experimented with shorter workdays with notable success.

So at the start of the COVID-19 crisis, we decided to formally amend the Michael Hyatt & Co. workday to six hours a day—as an experiment. We already had flexible hours, but we wanted to officially hem in the workday to make sure our team had the time they needed to deal with the extraordinary circumstances of the novel coronavirus.

What we discovered is that the shorter workday not only

encouraged greater focus, it also encouraged new and creative ways of approaching work altogether.

Constraints Foster Creativity

From early childhood, Phil Hansen aspired to be an artist. He attended art school and specialized in the pointillism style, a fragmenting technique that uses hundreds and thousands of tiny dots to form an image.

Over time, Hansen experienced severe nerve damage, causing his hand to shake. No longer was he capable of making perfectly round dots. Instead, his dots looked more like tadpoles. To compensate, he held his pen tighter—which only served to amplify his joint pain and suffering. Hansen felt like he was being robbed of his career, robbed of his dream. Distraught by this turn of events, Hansen abandoned his art for three full years. But he couldn't deny his calling.

Hansen decided to see a neurologist to check whether something could be done about the shake. Alas, no. The nerve damage was permanent. But his neurologist offered a suggestion: Why not just embrace the shake?

Upon returning home, Hansen took pencil to canvas and let his hand shake and shake and shake, ultimately producing drawings with squiggly lines. "Even though it wasn't the kind of art that I was ultimately passionate about," he later said in a TED Talk about his journey, "I realized I could still make art. I just had to find a different approach to making the art that I wanted."[10]

While the shake prohibited the creation of art with perfectly formed pointillist dots, that constraint forced him to experiment with other methods to fragment his images. Here's what he discovered: "If I worked on a larger scale and with bigger materials, my hand really wouldn't hurt, and after having gone from a single approach to art, I ended up having an approach to creativity that completely changed my artistic horizons. This was the first time I'd encountered this idea that embracing a limitation could actually drive creativity."[11]

Take his portrait of martial arts legend Bruce Lee. Using nothing more than the side of his hands dipped in black paint, Hansen applied strokes of paint to the canvas with karate chops. After that success, he explored other limitations. He asked himself, for instance, what might he create if he could spend only a dollar on art supplies? Or what might he create if he painted on his torso instead of on a canvas?

"Looking at limitations as a source of creativity changed the course of my life," he said. "Now, when I run into a barrier . . . I continue to show up for the process and try to remind myself of the possibilities."[12] This same game-changing principle applies to business as it does to art.

"Managers can innovate better by embracing constraints," according to researcher Oguz Acar and his colleagues. After reviewing 145 empirical studies on the impact of constraints on innovation and creativity, they reported that "individuals, teams, and organizations alike benefit from a healthy dose of constraints."[13]

How can placing limits enhance the results of our work? The research team found workers without constraints take the easiest route to the solution. "Complacency sets in," they said. In that state, "they go for the most intuitive idea that comes to mind rather than investing in the development of better ideas."[14]

Along that line, research by Rider University psychologist Catrinel Haught-Tromp shows employing constraints "allows a deeper exploration of fewer alternatives" because they "limit the overwhelming number of available choices to a manageable subset." In turn, she notes, this allows us to "explore less familiar paths, to diverge in previously unknown directions."[15] That's what our client Tiffany discovered when she decided to restrict her workday and workweek.

Constraints Drive Productivity

The cult of overwork doesn't distinguish between tasks. It just wants us to do more and gut it out. But that's a recipe for burnout. Like a lot of entrepreneurs, Tiffany was doing a bit of everything—and everything never ends.

When she and Paul joined our coaching program, they began to change the way they worked, focusing not on working more hours but on what kind of work they did within those hours. "I had never really sat down and looked at the big picture," she said. "It helps you to pick out those things where you can actually make the most progress—the things that you're good at, and not only the things you're good at, but the things that you are passionate about. It really helps you identify where you can make the progress and where you'll *enjoy* making the progress."

> The cult of overwork doesn't distinguish between tasks. It just wants us to do more and gut it out.

She began structuring her business around her own needs and interests, leaning in to tasks she loved and was skilled at doing and eliminating, automating, and delegating the rest. That change made all the difference. Not only was she able to break free of overwork, she also was able to break the ceiling on the company's growth. Instead of flat or marginal gains, in two years they grew their business more than 60 percent while working fewer, not more, hours. That's the kind of math we all need.

We've seen the same with our shorter workday at Michael Hyatt & Co. By cutting the day off at six hours, our team is more engaged and productive, constantly evaluating the work they're doing or might do against the daily cutoff. It encourages more and better planning, as well as eliminating nonessential activity.

Enhanced performance is one of the key outcomes of shorter workdays and workweeks when tried. Companies that have experimented with constrained work hours report better collaboration and ready adoption of labor-saving tools and techniques, along with greater focus and concentration. And as Alex Soojung-Kim Pang points out in his book *Shorter*—an exploration of constrained workdays and workweeks—those improvements have led directly to higher profits.[16]

Of course, workers win as well. Shorter hours mean we're free to focus on the other domains of life. "A shorter workday," Pang explains, "creates a clear incentive for individual innovation and a great opportunity to benefit directly from the improvements you make to a company's efficiency."[17] Normally, the work product of employees belongs to the company. Whatever gains or improvements they make might be rewarded in the form of commissions, bonuses, or perks. But that's not a given.

It's different when you're working to free up time. "Shortening the workday," says Pang, "isn't like adding to the corporate bottom line: a change you make shows results almost immediately and pays out in the form of time savings that everybody enjoys."[18] Time is money, and letting workers keep the savings is a powerful incentive to greater productivity and innovation, which then generate greater profits.

Making Changes

Embracing constraints prompts us to explore new and inventive ways of approaching our work, solving problems, completing projects, and more. Instead of doing it the way we always have—when we were working fifty-plus hours—we develop new ways of getting the work done. Or, and this is even better, we sometimes discover higher-leverage work, work with a higher return, and are able to abandon less advantageous labor.

That's exactly what Tiffany did. It caused her businesses to grow while still providing more margin for the rest of her life. By utilizing constraints, Tiffany has come to see that work and life operate as a symbiotic whole. Work gives you confidence, joy, and financial provision to bring home, and investing in your health, hobbies, and home life nurtures a clear mind and rested body to bring to work.

As Warren Buffett says, "The difference between successful people and really successful people is that really successful people say 'no' to almost everything."[19] Simply put, if you don't constrain your work, there won't be sufficient margin to engage in restorative activities like a proper vacation—or a peaceful evening, restful weekend, or much else. On the other hand, if you do constrain your work, you'll have the margin to invest in the activities that will ultimately drive better operating results in your business.

If you want to win with your business *and* succeed in the rest of your life, the secret lies in constraining labor to make room for the rest of your life. If you apply yourself to this, the life you will have six months from now, or a year from now, will be better, richer, and more satisfying than what you're experiencing today.

If you want to **win** with your business *and* **succeed** in the rest of your life, the secret lies in **constraining labor** to make room for the **rest** of your life.

Constrain Your Workday

So, when will you work and when won't you? That's the question to answer. Imagine your day is a twenty-four-ounce glass. Let's then say you have three basic liquids with which to fill the glass: achievement, nonachievement, and rest.

In this context, achievement mostly refers to work. Non-achievement refers to socializing, parenting, playing, hobbies, or just checking out (by the way, we'll cover nonachievement in depth in chapter 6). What about commuting? It depends on the person. Some use it for achievement, others for nonachievement. There's a difference between calling clients and listening to a novel. How you use that time is up to you. And rest, of course, primarily means sleep (more on that, by the way, in chapter 7).

Your glass won't get any bigger. Like time, it's fixed. But you can change the ratio of your ingredients that fill it as much as you like. The cult of overwork insists on filling the day with achievement. But since the capacity of the glass doesn't change, this leaves diminished room for nonachievement and rest. For a lot of high achievers, their glass looks like the illustration on the following page.

If these ingredients were a cocktail, these proportions would be tough to swallow, especially on a regular basis. We can also gulp down an extra dose of achievement when we need to, but

not continually. The Double Win suggests a different recipe—several different recipes, in fact, depending on your personal taste and needs. You can tinker with amounts to suit your situation, but we advise starting with roughly equal parts achievement, nonachievement, and rest. A well-balanced glass looks like this:

For people with the discretion and flexibility to manage it, we'd recommend even more nonachievement and rest time, which will

naturally edge down the amount of time dedicated to work or achievement. Why? As we saw earlier in this chapter, knowledge work is extremely demanding; six hours a day is an upper limit for most knowledge workers.

The most important part of constraining your workday is setting hard edges at the top and bottom of the day. You might find it desirable to add some padding in the middle of the day for a longer lunch, walk, or nap. That's always an option. But the start and stop of the workday are essential. For some that looks like taking no meetings before 9:00 or 9:30 in the morning, allowing time for a workday startup ritual (see Michael's book *Free to Focus*, pp. 119–20). It might look like taking no meetings after four o'clock in the afternoon.

A workday shutdown ritual is similarly helpful. It enables you to tie up loose ends before you leave. Instead of having a dozen things you still have to nail down when you get home, you're free to be present.

What might a bounded workday look like for you? Whatever you come up with, you'll need to share it with your team, clients, and boss. Be sure to sell vested parties on why it's in their best interest to support your boundaries. This is where we usually go wrong when setting boundaries. We just tell people, "I'm available only between 9:00 and 4:30." The end. That doesn't usually go over very well. Instead, we have to figure out why it's in *their* best interest to honor our boundaries and convince them of the point. If you're going to win at work and succeed at life, you've got to advocate for it.

Roy, one of our coaching clients, did this. He initially experienced some pushback from his colleagues. "We had a number of intense conversations at first," he told us. "They were concerned if they couldn't get me at 6:00 in the morning or at 7:00 at night to manage some issue because they were on a flight somewhere and needed to talk right away. I challenged them to measure me by the things that matter—one of those metrics was team retention. You know, whether or not my team is satisfied and are sticking with me for a long time. Secondly, I told them to measure me on whether I'm generating more gross profit dollars for the company than anyone else in the region. If the answer was yes to both of them, then I told them to leave me alone and let me do my job." His colleagues have honored his boundaries and, Roy says, "So far I've delivered on those results."

That said, a final caveat is in order. You have to be willing to make occasional exceptions to these boundaries. You want to shoot for holding the line here about 90 percent of the time, because real emergencies do occur. People will be far more supportive of your boundaries if they know you're willing to accommodate true emergencies when they arise. We want to be firm but not rigid.

It's kind of like the shocks on a car. They're firm but flexible, and that enables them to absorb the bumps in the road. As long as the results you're producing don't suffer, and if your boss and your clients know your *why*, usually they'll honor your boundaries. If they don't, maybe it's time to find a new boss or a new set of clients—those who share your win-win commitment to success.

5

THE PROMISE OF BALANCE

Work-Life Balance Is Truly Possible

We spend too much of our work lives trying to deny our humanity.

RICHARD SHERIDAN[1]

Few things make me (Megan) happier than a steaming bowl of pad thai. There's a place nearby Joel and I like to go for date nights. He gets curry. I get pad thai. The first time we went, I didn't even need to look at the menu. I knew exactly what I wanted. I'd been craving it for weeks. The waiter came to our table with her order pad and pencil.

"Have you decided what you'll order?" she asked.

"I'll have the pad thai," I said, also requesting some spring rolls.

"What number for the pad thai," she asked, "1 to 5?"

"What do the numbers mean?"

"How spicy you want it—1 is the least spicy, 5 is the most."

I stopped to consider my answer. I do like things spicy, though not as spicy as Joel; he orders way too hot for my taste. But I don't like it bland either. It's not pad thai without some kick. I figured I'd take the Goldilocks approach, not too weak, not too spicy. "I'll have the 3."

We were through with our spring rolls and deep in conversation when the entrees arrived. I was excited. I took in the steam with its smell of cilantro, peanuts, and sauce. I squeezed a wedge of lime on top and twirled some noodles on my fork. The first bite was amazing. Then, without warning, my hair was on fire. Holy cow, that was hot! And the spice just kept getting more intense. My lips started stinging. My eyes started watering. Were there scorch marks on my cheeks?

I tried another bite, but I wasn't sure I could keep going. I didn't want to reject the food. This wasn't the restaurant's fault. They're completely competent making the dishes they offer. But the heat, at least for my taste, was totally out of balance. Lesson learned. The next time I ordered 1. It was perfect.

Missing the Point

Balance is everything. But it's fashionable to dismiss or even attack the concept these days. Some call it a fantasy, others call it a myth. "There is no such thing," says one pundit. "In fact, I'd go so far as to say that the very idea is an insidious lie."[2] One *Forbes* contributor describes the pursuit of work-life balance as "this generation's version of the pursuit of the fountain of youth."[3] Another writer calls it a "frustrating and useless idea."[4]

Maria Popova is the force behind *Brain Pickings*, one of the most consistently thought-provoking sites on the internet. "I often find myself saddened when people talk of 'work-life balance,'" she says, "a notion that implies we need to counter the unpleasantness we endure in order to make a living with the pleasurable activities we long to do in order to feel alive."[5]

We think she's misdiagnosed the problem. Work is good. In fact, there's so much goodness in work that we have to be intentional about giving other aspects of life their due.

Our concern is that saying work-life balance is a myth—or worse—becomes the camel's nose under the tent flap of overwork. We see that in the lives of people we coach. As we make peace with the fact that balance is hard to maintain, we make temporary compromises that shortchange the other

> **There's so much goodness in work that we have to be intentional about giving other aspects of life their due.**

domains of life. If we're not committed to balance, those compromises can easily become full-fledged patterns of practice.

Consider lifestyle maven Martha Stewart. "It's one of the most difficult things to do; that balance, which is so elusive to most of us, it didn't work for me," she told CNN. "I had to sacrifice a marriage because of the lure of the great job. It's impossible for most of us to get that balance."[6]

Maybe detractors believe balance is a myth because, like Popova, they have a wrong view of what balance looks like.

Understanding Balance

Years ago, I (Michael) took a group on a ropes course. It might sound like a hokey team-alignment exercise, but it was actually a great experience. Most of our focus was on learning how to balance. To do this, our host strung ropes between several tree trunks, twelve inches off the ground. All we risked was a sprained ankle and some embarrassment, but we found it super challenging.

We had several valuable takeaways. First, balancing and walking on a tightrope is one thing when you're doing it alone. As soon as you add another person—or several persons—the difficulty factor increases exponentially. Second, we had to learn how to hold on to each other as we worked our way across the line. We were constantly counterbalancing each other as we moved forward. That required communication and coordination.

Third, and what I remember most of all, when we were balanced, it never really felt like we were balanced. Our legs constantly moved and wobbled; we strained to grip each other and the nearest tree. But we stayed on that line a long time by making little corrections, adjusting our weight, trying to stay upright. If we were static, we'd fall down every time.

Balance requires constant effort. We were in the least danger when we made adjustments to the imbalance we felt.

With intentionality and practice, nobody needed to fall off. And that's exactly how life is.

It's a mistake to believe that you will ever reach a season in life when you can evenly distribute your time, energy, and focus, so you're spending the same amount of time at work as in your personal life. That is never going to happen. Nor is that the goal. Instead, the key is to spend the *appropriate* amount of time in each of the major categories of life. That looks different in different times and seasons.

Here are three vital aspects of balance to keep in mind, especially as we apply the concept to our work and life:

Balance is not the same as rest. When people we coach talk about their need for more balance, what they're really saying is that they're stressed, overwhelmed, worn out, and in need of an extended period of rest. We get that. But if we think attaining balance means finally getting a much-needed break, then we're missing something important. Balance is not about rest, though it does include rest, because without proper rest, productivity and efficiency suffer.

Balance is about *distributing demands* so we can stay on track with a win at work and at life. We don't want to cannibalize one sphere of life to feed the other. That takes intentionality. Don't be discouraged. It's just part of the challenge.

Balance is dynamic. "Life is like riding a bicycle," Albert Einstein said in a letter to his son Eduard. "To keep your balance you must keep moving."[7] We've all experienced this. The slower you go, the more trouble it is to keep your bike from wobbling until you crash. Momentum helps us stay upright and on course.

It's the same for all the corrections and adjustments we make along the way to stay balanced. Balance requires tweaking our schedule and task lists. If you have it right one week, it still requires attention the next week—or when unexpected developments arise. Inevitably, your boss will ask you to work late to finish a project; a child will fall sick, requiring your attention; your car will break down; or your plane will be canceled. Don't let that throw you for a loop. Like an athlete on the track, remind yourself you're in a marathon, not a sprint. Pace yourself with micro course corrections to maintain your stride.

Labor economist and Stanford business professor Myra Strober uses another analogy. "A rocket is exactly on target only at takeoff and landing," she says. "Between those two points, it constantly moves away from its trajectory and has to be 'straightened out.' So, too, with work and family. The two are rarely in balance, and each member of the couple needs to keep an eye out to discern when the imbalance requires correction."[8]

Balance is intentional. Our bodies are programmed to stay upright, but it takes a bit more focus when it comes to the complex responsibilities and relationships that make up our lives. We have to make purposeful decisions and actions if we want to maintain balance. It's not accidental. Those decisions and actions will look different for each of us, but they're essential for all of us to make, just the same.

When we say balance is intentional, that also means it's a "caused thing"—you make it happen. Balance isn't going to just show up at your doorstep and announce, "Here I am, you're all balanced and ready to go." Put another way, balance begins with your intention to create something different with your future. It's achievable, but you've got to formulate and articulate a plan to get to the future Double Win that you design.

Trade-Offs

Practically speaking, balance is about trade-offs. When you're working fifty-, sixty-, seventy-plus hours a week, you're putting at risk four important assets that could, if properly cared for, supercharge your success at the office. Conversely, neglecting them is to put yourself at risk for a wide range of unwanted consequences.

Trading your health. When you're starting your career, it's tempting to believe you can get by eating junk food rather than blocking the time to prepare or acquire a healthy meal. Likewise, it's easy to skip your exercise routine in favor of spending extra time on the job.

Dick Costolo, former CEO at Twitter, believes that's a shortsighted strategy. Even while running a global company with more than 200 million active users, he made time for regular exercise. "You'll get a much bigger return from twenty minutes of exercise than you will from another twenty minutes wading through emails or being in meetings," he says.[9]

Neglecting our health inevitably catches up with us. How many people do you know who have died young simply because they refused to take care of themselves? Of course, there are congenital diseases and other issues that cause people to die early. But at least some of our health problems are self-imposed.

Trading your family. We saw earlier that executives and entrepreneurs experience divorce at a greater rate than the rest of the workforce. The relational cost of overwork is incalculable. We're not talking just about spousal support, alimony, the division of assets, therapy, or the additional costs associated with shared parenting in two dwellings. Sometimes divorce is unavoidable. But if we can identify overwork as a key cause, then we can certainly address at least that.

And think about our kids. If you (like me, Michael) don't invest in them when they're young, you'll be forced to spend time with them later—in the principal's office, in a counselor's office, in rehab, or worse.

By contrast, studies demonstrate that a healthy marriage and family dynamic breathes life into your emotional well-being and personal satisfaction, as well as longevity.[10] Take time to enjoy your family when you can. These benefits are only realized by leveraging and protecting your family from overwork.

Trading your friends. As Aristotle said centuries ago, "In poverty and other misfortunes of life, true friends are a sure refuge. They keep the young out of mischief; they comfort and aid the old in their weakness; and they incite those in the prime of life to noble deeds."[11] Time and research have proven him right.

Sadly, I (Michael) didn't really have any close personal friends until about seven years ago. I hate to admit that. I had colleagues at work. But they were acquaintances, people I had a professional relationship with that I mistook for friendship. Those relationships are great as far as they go.

However, that's an entirely different dynamic than having deep friendships with people who don't have any agenda other than to love you, share in your joys, and comfort you in times of sorrow.

Good friends also have implications for improving health. According to the Mayo Clinic, "Friends also play a significant role in promoting your overall health. Adults with strong social support have a reduced risk of many significant health problems, including depression, high blood pressure and an unhealthy body mass index."[12] Thankfully, after designing my schedule around the principles of the Double Win, I now have cultivated those kinds of relationships, and I'm a better person for it.

Trading your effectiveness and productivity. Occasional stress can heighten performance, but when the strain of over-work is constant, it undermines it. Think of sports. In golf, the harder you work at your game, the tighter your grip, the more you bear down on your club, the more stressed you become. And your swing suffers as a result. It's the same with fly-fishing, or most anything.

Jim Loehr and Tony Schwartz, coauthors of *The Power of Full Engagement*, worked with professional athletes. They noticed when athletes began to get stressed and when they began to get tense, their performance would wane. They took what they learned from working with athletes and started applying it to professionals. They saw the same phenomenon. Constant stress undermined performance.

Constant stress leaves us unhappy, and that dings our productivity as well. A study authored by three economists at the University of Warwick found improved happiness

This abandonment of balance especially burdens women.

produced 12 percent improvement in productivity. Unhappy workers, on the other hand, were 10 percent less productive.[13]

Those are the four main assets you put at risk when you don't get this priority management thing in hand: Your health. Your family. Your friends. Your effectiveness.

Now, don't get us wrong. We work hard and sometimes screw up and get overcommitted. In pursuing balance, we have to be kind with ourselves. "A rocket is exactly on target only at takeoff and landing," to quote Myra Strober again. If you find yourself in a season where you're off-balance, consider the trade-offs and get back on track.

What concerns us most is the widely held assumption that you must abandon balance and sacrifice your personal wellness, family life, self-enrichment, emotional health, and spiritual wholeness just to be and stay competitive. This abandonment of balance especially burdens women.

Adam, Eve, and Don

"The day's hectic march." That's how CEO Jennifer Goldman-Wetzler describes the stretch between six in the morning and nine at night. "As with most working parents, each day is a delicate Rube Goldberg machine of moving parts," she says; "if I shift my attention away, missing one of the steps of the sequence, the ball drops and the game is over. At least it seems that way."[14]

I (Megan) know the feeling. Goldman-Wetzler speaks of working parents in general, but the challenge of getting it all done each day often falls unequally to women. Keynes was wrong about more than the fifteen-hour workweek.

While he joked about "the old Adam in most of us" getting all the work we needed in a few hours a day, he apparently never imagined Eve entering the workforce. But we have, and we're excelling. We're also struggling, as evidenced by the analysis of authors such as Brigid Schulte in her book *Overwhelmed* and Anne-Marie Slaughter in *Unfinished Business.*

Traditionally speaking, women have run the domestic sphere while men tackled a trade. As women entered the workforce, however, they retained their domestic commitments while adding professional ones. This means a full-time professional might put in fifty hours at the office, possibly more, while still trying to manage her home, kids, and all the rest: pediatrician appointments, meal planning, grocery shopping, cooking, school meetings, and laundry, laundry, laundry. To get it all done requires an incredible amount of planning and hustle. And if one piece slips out of place, like the Rube Goldberg machine, the day goes haywire.

When I (Michael) was first making my way in business I could count on Gail shouldering the domestic side of our lives. That was our unspoken deal. As I shared in chapters 1 and 2, I pushed it too far. Many men do. I can't imagine the burden of running a company *and* running a home. But many women do just that.

The majority of moms are now employed full-time, according to the Pew Research Center; just a third were employed full-time in 1968.[15] As of 2015, both mom and dad work full-time in almost half of homes.[16] Men tend to work more hours, but American Time Use Survey data shows full-time working moms spend three and a third more hours on childcare, do three and a half hours more housework, and get about four hours less leisure per week than do working dads.[17]

And leisure might be a bit of a stretch anyway. Women's leisure time, as Brigid Schulte points out, often involves a tremendous amount of work-like activity. "Women are typically the ones who plan, organize, pack, execute, delegate, and clean up after outings, holidays, vacations, and family events," she says. It's what moms do, right?

They also end up giving a lot of their leisure time to their kids, retaining only "interrupted scraps of time." Schulte mentions a study of thirty-two middle-class moms in Los Angeles whose leisure typically occurred in bursts of ten minutes or less.[18] Long periods to decompress and rejuvenate are hard to come by. That is true for men, as we've seen, but it seems more so for women.

The added burdens of home produce strains and stresses women would often like to escape. The psychologist whose observations on flow we explored in chapter 2, Mihaly Csikszentmihalyi, has noted that men are happier at home than women, whose mood improves at the office.

As Schulte reports on Csikszentmihalyi's findings, "Women . . . reported feeling happiest around midday, when most were at work, and felt the worst between 5:30 and 7:30 p.m." This is the block of time when the glow of flow vanishes, and it's all about picking up kids, figuring out dinner, overseeing homework, chores, evening routines, and the rest. "For women," says Schulte, "home, no matter how filled with love and happiness, is just another workplace."[19]

I (Megan) know that some people reading this might be tempted to dismiss it. But the uncomfortable truth is that social and economic norms have changed while cultural expectations lag somewhere behind. Women are left making up the difference.

Thankfully, these inequities are improving. Men today are far more willing to renegotiate traditional roles and responsibilities than their fathers. Joel and I have, for instance, shuffled and rearranged how we approach the kids, chores, and so on. But inequities are still present and problematic for countless women attempting to give their best at both home and the office, especially when we look beyond the troubles at home and see how work adds to the imbalance women experience.

> **Inequities are still present and problematic for countless women attempting to give their best at both home and the office.**

Schulte and others have pointed out that the picture of the ideal worker embedded in American work culture is a man with no real outside family responsibilities—someone who can put in ridiculous hours and sacrifice margin for the goals of the business. Michelle King, director of inclusion at Netflix, calls this the Don Draper ideal, after the character in the television hit series *Mad Men*.[20] Family men struggle to perform against this standard, but the challenge to women is greater still.

The answer to this problem is not abandoning balance like Martha Stewart and Don Draper, but (at least in part) for both women and men to fully embrace it. We're not saying it's easy. Cultural norms and office policy have inertia and resist change. What's more, they work like grooves we

ADAM   EVE   DON

can slip into and move along without any extra thought or effort. But balance, as we've seen, requires extra effort—starting with renegotiating the deal couples and companies have in place.

Another writer, who dismisses balance as something only acrobats can do, nonetheless tells the story of how Melanie Healey, a marketing manager for Procter & Gamble, renegotiated a better deal. Recently returned from maternity leave, Healey was offered a special assignment from her boss. A classic Don Draper type, he was famous for starting meetings before 7:00 a.m. and leaving late. That wouldn't work for Healey and her new baby.

She agreed to take the assignment as long as he agreed to her new hours. "I am going to get here at eight in the morning. So you can't start a meeting before eight," she told him. "I am going to be home at six o'clock. So you can't start a meeting after five that doesn't end by five to six so I can be home by six." The boss was surprised by her demands but didn't want to lose her help. He agreed.[21]

Striking a new balance is possible. The trouble is, we fail to achieve it because we don't always believe so and thus never even try.

Two Words of Caution

First, when we talk about winning at work and succeeding at life, it doesn't mean everything is perfect. There is no ideal combo of job, family, rest, and hobbies, and you're not home free if you find it. That's magical thinking.

Sometimes we feel imbalanced even when we're doing well, because balance requires tension, which can be tough to maintain. The mistake is when we resolve the tension by going all in on work (the Hustle Fallacy) or underserve our work to focus on home (the Ambition Brake). The tension might cause strain, but it's part of the dynamism that makes balance possible in the first place. Once we adjust our perspective, we can see balance for what it is: a challenging but rewarding way to approach our lives.

Winning at work and succeeding at life doesn't mean you have the final say over all the outcomes in your life. It means prioritizing what you should prioritize, influencing what you can influence, and controlling what you can control. You don't always have control over the outcomes because they involve other people. But you do have control over what you choose to focus on and how.

It's narcissistic to think you control all the outcomes in your life. You could do everything perfectly in terms of your health and still get cancer. You could do everything right as a parent and still end up with a kid addicted to drugs, in jail, or committing suicide. You could do everything right in terms of your marriage and still end up with a divorce, your spouse dying early, or whatever. If success means perfection, then we're all out of luck.

Thankfully, it doesn't mean that. When we talk about the

Double Win, we mean having freedom to prioritize what matters most to you in all the important domains of your life. We mean doing life as much as possible on your own terms. We mean investing in the people and priorities that are most meaningful to you, while recognizing that the return on that investment isn't always or exactly up to you.

Second, we need to remember the reasons for overwork covered in chapter 2. A lot of times we're out of balance and we don't want to change because imbalance gives us a sense of significance. We deceive ourselves by holding on to the belief that "I'm so important because I'm in such demand. I'm required to be out of balance."

We might have to lean into a project for a few days or weeks to bring it in on time. We might have to defer fully engaging other life domains for periods of time to attend to those that need attention most in the moment. If you're diagnosed with cancer, you'd better attend to that. If your child needs

> **When we talk about the Double Win, we mean having freedom to prioritize what matters most to you in all the important domains of your life.**

extra attention, don't question the trade-off; just do it. But if work continues to throw you off-balance, maybe it's not as important as you think. You might just be falling for one of the reasons for overwork.

The important thing to note is that you have agency. You can create a different outcome if you really want to make the change. If you're in an onerous situation affecting your work-life balance, to the point where you're not giving attention to things you know you should give attention to, such as your health and family, then set a goal to get out of that job.

The change might not be today, this week, or even this year, but come up with an exit strategy so that you can have a life. Design your life the way you want it to be. That's always a possibility. You have options. The question is, do you have the imagination and desire to change?

DOUBLE WIN PRACTICE

Schedule What Matters

When we talk to our clients about work-life balance, we often hear that their calendars are full of everyone else's priorities but theirs. It's easy to let happen. The always-on work culture can rob us of our margin. When colleagues and clients expect responses to emails at all hours, it's hard to make room for socializing or even sleep.

Sometimes we do it to ourselves. We're eager to accept new opportunities. Maybe we're in one of those "make hay while the sun shines" seasons of our career, or we just want to be helpful to people. Maybe there's an opportunity at church to be on a committee or to volunteer, or you're asked to serve on a special committee at school. Before you know it, the calendar gets packed with everyone's wins but your own.

The solution is to proactively schedule your own priorities. In the last chapter, we talked about constraining your workday. Now it's time to look at the week, and not just the workweek. Balance requires that we need to get clarity on the whole thing.

The week is like the drinking glass of chapter 4's Double Win practice. It's got hard edges that define and constrain the time we have. Each week has 168 hours. How will you fill them? Here are some suggestions on how to answer that question for yourself and implement your answer.

    Plan an Ideal Week. To plan an Ideal Week, you need a blank template of seven days. We recommend arranging the days Monday through Sunday. That's how we have it in our Full Focus Planner. But Sunday through Saturday or another combination can work equally well. Now think in blocks of time. What goes where?

    If you remember the nonnegotiables we talked about in chapter 3, you've already got the key groupings: self-care, relational priorities, and professional results. You can also look to the ten life domains in chapter 3 to make sure you don't leave anything out. Because you've already constrained your day, you know

THE IDEAL WEEK

	MON	TUE	WED	THU	FRI	SAT	SUN
8:00	Morning Routine						
9:00	Workday Startup						
10:00	Deep Work						Church
11:00	Deep Work						Church
12:00	Lunch					House Chores	Family
1:00	Team Mtgs	Team Mtgs			External Mtgs	House Chores	Family
2:00	Team Mtgs	Team Mtgs			External Mtgs	House Chores	Family
3:00	Team Mtgs	Team Mtgs			External Mtgs	House Chores	Family
4:00	Team Mtgs	Team Mtgs			External Mtgs	House Chores	Family
5:00	Workday Shutdown						
6:00	Exercise				Date Night	Friends	
7:00	Dinner				Date Night	Friends	
8:00	Free Time					Friends	
9:00	Free Time					Friends	
10:00	Go to Bed						

when work starts and stops. If your workday takes up six, seven, eight hours a day, you've got a fair bit of margin to play with. The idea is to schedule the kind of activities outside of work hours that will provide you with the balance you want.

For instance, if you want to save one night a week for seeing friends, block it on your Ideal Week. Unpredictable schedules are a key reason we socialize less these days than in prior times.[22] When our evenings are compressed because of last-minute meetings or dotted with random work assignments, it's hard to make plans in advance with friends and others. But if you know that, say, Thursday evenings are set aside for drinks or dinner, you can schedule without worry you'll have to cancel, or miss out because you weren't confident enough about your schedule to plan in the first place.

This works also for regular bedtime, waketime, exercise, yoga, date nights, family dinner, church, meditation, walks, whatever. Block the time and make it happen. The predictability ensures greater odds for success.

Preview the coming week. We're more likely to keep our balance if we proactively keep our eyes on what's coming. That's why we also recommend previewing the week, preferably with your spouse or partner if you have one. Take time before the week begins to look at deadlines, commitments, events, and so on. Parent-teacher meetings, doctor's appointments, client dinners, and the rest don't come from nowhere. But sometimes we forget about them or only one party in the relationship knows about them.

This is a chance to get clear on expectations; who's doing what and when. Balance is much easier to manage when we rule out surprises. We have a tool in the Full Focus Planner for this as well, but you can do this with whatever calendar or planning tool you favor.

Schedule the specifics when you can. Nature abhors a vacuum. So does work. One of the challenges with weekends and why we can lose our balance and overwork is that we don't know what else to do with ourselves. Along with planning general blocks of time with your Ideal Week, you'll also want to plan individual days, especially weekend ones. (You can do that with a Full Focus Planner as well, but again it's not required.)

For many of us, it's second nature to treat Saturday as a catch-up day or Sunday as a jump-start day. That's all the more so if we don't have something else scheduled. The reasons for overwork covered in chapter 2 are still true on the weekends, and the draw of the unread reports, unanswered emails, or unwritten brief can pull us away from restful and rejuvenating time with friends, family, or ourselves.

Give yourself a break. Some people are fine leaving the day open and letting it take its course. But others benefit from scheduling the specific activities. Fix the car with a friend, tackle a home-improvement project, get your nails done, or go hiking with the family. If it helps you follow through, schedule it just like you would a meeting with your most important client.

6

A PROFITABLE PAUSE

—————— PRINCIPLE 4 ——————
There's Incredible Power
in Nonachievement

You are not a to-do list.

ROBERT POYNTON[1]

In 1990 J.K. Rowling boarded a crowded train to travel from Manchester to London's King's Cross. Somewhere midroute, the train rumbled to a stop. She and the other passengers waited. And waited. Four hours passed before the train continued its journey. Would you blame her if she fumed at the delay? Four hours sitting anywhere not achieving anything, let alone on a gloomy train, would be enough to push even a seasoned traveler over the edge.

117

Not so with Rowling. Her window of nonachievement gave rise to a new character named Harry Potter who, according to her website, just "fell into her head" while she was stuck on the train. "I had been writing almost continuously since the age of six but I had never been so excited about an idea before," Rowling reflected. "I did not have a functioning pen with me, but I do think that this was probably a good thing. I simply sat and thought, for four (delayed train) hours, while all the details bubbled up in my brain, and this scrawny, black-haired, bespectacled boy who didn't know he was a wizard became more and more real to me."[2]

Pause for a moment. She had no pen! Ideas can slip away as fast as they appear. It must have been maddening to have such an incredible inspiration with no way of jotting it down. Never mind the challenge of tuning out a stalled train full of distractions—murmuring fellow passengers miffed about the delay, rustling newspapers, parents tending to bored and complaining children, and all the rest.

Somehow she held the inspiration and hammered out a synopsis and sample chapter when she got home. A dozen publishers passed on the story, but Rowling eventually found a publisher who understood what she was trying to do. She signed a deal with a $5,000 advance the publisher has long since recouped.

That unexpected four-hour window of nonachievement was Rowling's golden ticket. The first printing of *Harry Potter and the Philosopher's Stone* was only 500 hardback copies. Today the Harry Potter series has sold over 500 million copies. It's been translated into 80 languages, has spawned eight major movies, plus spinoffs, and has produced more than $7 billion in licensed merchandise. According to the

Financial Times, Rowling's brand has been valued at more than $25 billion.[3]

I (Michael) have been involved in publishing thousands of books during my tenure as book marketer, publisher, and CEO. I've had my share of *New York Times* bestsellers and runaway hits. But I never had a title or series of titles take off like it's got one of Elon Musk's rockets tied on back. Rowling's achievement lives in rarified air.

But what's important to recognize in Rowling's story is the direct relationship between her results and being stuck with nothing to do on a train going nowhere. It's exciting to contemplate her achievement and all the doing that went into it. But there's more to doing than action.

No pause, no profit. If you want to win the race, you have to put the car in neutral now and then. But we don't easily accept that, do we?

The Need to Achieve

After weeks of preparation and months of hustle, what does the boss ask? "Did we achieve the goal?" Answer yes, and the individual, team, or division enjoys the praise that comes with success. Bigger budgets and additional staff tend to follow the triumph, since smart companies pour gasoline on the business units producing results. Answer no, however, and you might be looking at scowls, tirades, or worse. Miss often enough and big enough, and you're looking at budget cuts, reassignments, dismissals, and layoffs.

The block-and-tackle of business—vision-casting, strategies, forecasts, spreadsheets, timelines, metrics, outcomes, and so on—all have achievement in view. We're hardwired to pursue return on investment, and we obtain it only when we achieve what we set out to accomplish. And there's good reason for that. Without achievement, business stagnates and companies fail. Leadership knows achievement is essential to survival. Which is why bonuses are paid when we achieve, not when we try.

I (Michael) have an almost insatiable drive to achieve. I'm the kind of guy who constantly checks the metrics to ensure I'm beating last month's numbers, no matter what they are. I love succeeding. This can get pathological; I already mentioned that early in my career I used to open my office door at five o'clock in the morning and lock it again at six in the evening. I was desperate to achieve.

If we're not careful, our identity and self-worth can be so enmeshed in our role and in the accolades of achievement that our life lacks meaning without it. This is the dark side of work being a primary means of self-actualization (see chapter 2). When we achieve, we feel useful, fulfilled, upbeat, and positive. Conversely, when we don't achieve, we feel like failures.

We get a biting sense that high performers on the team will upstage us, steal the spotlight, and get the promotion—maybe even our job. While extolling the value of overwork, Elon Musk said as much, remember? When you put in twice the hours, he said, you get twice as much done. Of course, that's not true. There are diminishing returns, and productivity goes backward after about fifty hours on the job. But he was playing on our fears—and our thrills. Work is a competition! You don't want to lose! You could be winning! Work more and win!

But that myopic focus on achievement means we miss the benefits of nonachievement. The cult of overwork says a person should be always busy, achieving something. We endorse this view by actively trying to fill up the hours with work or fidgeting and fussing when we don't. But, as with its other tenets, the cult of overwork is wrong as can be.

The Necessity of White Space

We have a friend who runs a print shop with industrial-sized printing equipment. His machines are state of the art, but as he points out, they can't run 100 percent of the time. Full capacity for a printing press looks like operating 85 percent of the time, with 15 percent downtime necessary for maintenance.

It's the same with people, only more so. Kids have recess at school, and adults similarly need breaks to stay productive. We need a rhythm of work and rest to be our best at work and at home. Our brains and bodies are not designed for constant work. We need periods of nonachievement.

As we saw in chapter 2, achievement is about the end purpose of the activity, the accomplished goal, the completed project, the checked-off task. But nonachievement activities are about themselves. We drink wine to enjoy it. We laugh through an evening with friends to enjoy their company. We play an instrument to enjoy making music.

We need a rhythm of work and rest to be our best at work and at home.

We do those things to *do* them—to experience them in the moment. That present-tense activity involves other parts of our being. It allows the always-on part to rest and asks other (usually more reluctant) parts to come out and play. And we feel better when we do.

Many of the most enriching, restorative activities in our lives are not about ROI: hobbies, art, friendships, music, cocktails, crafts, games, book clubs, walking a stretch of beach, or just ambling outside for thirty minutes. Pursuits like these are restorative, rejuvenating, recharging. And they do so precisely because they are not geared toward achievement.

Some of us feel uncomfortable disengaging from work. Because of our always-on culture, we might feel guilty letting an email that came in at eight at night go unanswered until the following morning.[4] One CEO talked to *Inc.* magazine about his typical workday, which is packed with planning and meetings. When he finally gets home more than twelve hours after leaving in the morning, he spends time with his kids, eats dinner with the family, then watches TV and catches up with his wife. But, he admits, "I keep an eye on my phone for work stuff, which I know is bad."[5]

This CEO is not alone. Recall from chapter 2 that professionals tend to not only work excessively long hours but also monitor their work even once they're technically finished for the day or week. Try as we might, hitting the pause button is hard.

We often use words like *white space* and *margin* to talk about spare time. The terms come from the world of printing and publishing. I (Michael) spent practically my whole career in the publishing business. But you don't need decades of experience to get the key point. Any casual reader knows it just as well. A page so crowded with words that there's no white space, no margin, is unreadable. The same is true for life. As we crowd it with tasks, activities, and busyness, we make it less livable.

In chapter 3 we talked about nonnegotiables. The white space is where two of those—self-care and relationships—usually fit best. And we do have some natural margin built into the week, particularly nights and weekends. But the cult of overwork has eroded those hours.

Like the CEO above, we regularly check email after hours when we could be chatting with our family or friends, going for a walk, relaxing with a book, catching up on a show, or whatever else. Four in ten American employees check work email after eleven at night, according to a GFI Software survey. And while weekends afford more time for rest, recreation, and the like, GFI found 74 percent of workers nonetheless monitor their inbox over the weekend.[6] It's time off, but we're still on. Our face is in our phone, and work is on our mind.

Your Brain Is Never Off—Just Differently On

Our brains are always working. The question is, what are they working on? Periods of nonachievement allow other parts of our brains to operate, and this pays tremendous dividends. In fact, psychologist and Kellogg School of Management associate professor Adam Waytz calls leisure our killer app.

Discussing the present and future disruptions caused by AI to the job market, Waytz asks what humans can do that computers can't. For one thing, he says, while our minds wander, computer processors don't. If we're thinking about focusing on the work right in front of us, that might be good.

A wandering mind might forget to respond to that important Slack message, might struggle to finish the monthly financial report, might miss a key point in a meeting. But there are benefits to a wandering mind too. And downtime helps us access them.

Strong connections exist between mind wandering and creative thinking, lateral problem solving, and generating unique ideas. "By encouraging our minds to wander, leisure activities pull us out of our present reality, which in turn can improve our ability to generate novel ideas or ways of thinking," he says. "When we let our minds drift away from work, we return to our tasks capable of tackling them in more inventive creative ways."[7]

Our brains are never off, just differently on. That means they're still working in the background, noodling away. Some writers use the trick of finishing their writing for the day with an incomplete sentence because the brain keeps working on it; when they start up again the following day, their mind is already on the job. The period of rest allows for rejuvenation without detracting from the work; rather, it contributes to it.

"Neither constant stress nor monotony is a very good context for creativity," says Mihaly Csikszentmihalyi, the psychologist who popularized the concept of flow, introduced in chapter 2. "You should alternate periods of stress with periods of relaxation." Relaxation could be time to just sit and reflect, which Csikszentmihalyi suggests. But he also says our minds wander in creative directions when we walk, swim, garden, shower, and do crafts. To that list we can add cooking, fishing, golfing, and other such activities. Csikszentmihalyi says rock climbing, skiing, or skydiving can work as well. The trick is doing something that takes you out of your work context and plunges you into something altogether different.[8]

The problem with overworking is that we marginalize or utterly miss these periods of profitable pause, where we can put other parts of our minds and bodies to use, and thereby benefit from use of our whole person, instead of the aspect most focused on work.

History, business case studies, and magazine profiles are replete with stories of innovations, solutions, products, even whole companies, born out of periods of nonachievement. And a surprising number of our Michael Hyatt & Co. clients have likewise experienced breakthrough innovations, solutions to complex problems, or complete career changes leading to a happier, healthier life once their ideas had a chance to percolate during a period of nonachievement.

Time-Out

Our client Amy had her eureka moment as a result of a two-week self-imposed nonachievement break, something she did out of desperation.

At the time, Amy was a driven high achiever, working full-time for a nonprofit counseling center, while attending graduate school and raising a family. Studying late into the evening, shortchanging sleep, prepping kids for school in the morning, heading to work for the day, and then stumbling home in time to make dinner was her norm.

After three years of juggling her impossible, marginless schedule, Amy recognized her routine was just about "killing my family . . . it was *bad*." Worse, she was convinced that she wasn't doing what she really wanted to do with her life and was ready to throw in the towel. She even thought she was headed for a mental breakdown. Amy told her husband, "I might need to be hospitalized, I think I am so depressed."

That's when she took a two-week vacation. She'd never done that before. Like far too many high achievers, she was convinced extended time away was a pipe dream. We know exactly how she felt. Most of our careers we felt guilty if we weren't working during vacation. We felt we were being lazy and, in a way, letting our company down.

During her vacation, Amy didn't sip lemonade under palm trees overlooking an ocean view. She didn't plan a grand adventure to the Bahamas or some other exotic corner of the world. Rather, Amy instinctively knew she lacked clarity and decided to do nothing but sit idly in her backyard for a two-week staycation. She forced herself off the treadmill to get in touch with what was driving her at a deeper level.

"I sat in the backyard and cried for three days," she said. "I sent my kids off to school in the morning, and then I would literally sit there in my backyard doing nothing all day. I would move to maybe eat lunch, but that's it. I would still be there when the kids got home."

She admitted feeling lost for the first week. She decided journaling might help. "I wrote random thoughts at first," she said, "a word here, a sentence there." It took a while to find her way through the mire of conflicting emotions and difficult thoughts. But as she reread the random thoughts in her journal, she began to see patterns. That's when the aha! moment hit.

"I was reminded that I've owned my own business before," she said. "Suddenly the truth started coming out of me. I discovered it wasn't the counseling profession that I wanted to quit. It's the working-for-somebody-else part that I wanted to quit. I still was very interested in helping people."

She didn't sit on the revelation. "I looked up counseling space for rent—just for myself. I found a place and made a phone call. The landlord said he was actually there and to come over if I wanted to take a look. He had just one space left. When I got there, I literally wrote the guy a check in the parking lot. I hadn't even told my husband yet! That decision came out of my sitting in my backyard long enough to discover what was most important to me."

Two forces were working against Amy, both resulting from her whirlwind of achievement. First, she'd lost sight of her nonnegotiables (chapter 3). Instead of staying focused on the professional results she was best suited to deliver, she'd taken on tasks for which she lacked passion and proficiency. (For more on the vital intersection of these two, see Michael's book *Free to Focus*.)

Second, in the constant blur, Amy was unable to find time for self-reflection. "The space and quiet that idleness provides is a necessary condition for standing back from life and seeing it whole," says cartoonist Tim Kreider, "for making unexpected connections and waiting for the wild summer lightning strikes of inspiration—it is, paradoxically, necessary to getting any work done."[9]

Indeed, once Amy carved out time to be idle, lightning struck and the impact was career- and life-changing. "The decision to branch out on my own was huge," says Amy. "I thought it was just going to be me practicing therapy on my own. But I quickly had more clients than I could handle. I grew from just me to a team of sixteen counselors in only two years, with my business generating seven figures. I also have an online component with an additional support staff of five—and we're getting ready to hire two more this month. If I hadn't sat in my backyard doing nothing for two weeks, I probably would still be unhappily working for someone else."

Today, Amy is living the Double Win because she put herself in "time-out" long enough to get reacquainted with her true passion.

Grounded in Newark

For twenty years, Tamara, an ambitious high achiever, was a process engineer at Verizon. Tamara implemented large-scale projects designed to improve processes, eliminate waste, and increase profitability. "I would go into a failing division of the organization and assess it to decide how we could improve the processes and turn it into a more profitable division," Tamara told us. Most of her projects saved the company several million dollars.

For years she was required to travel 75 percent of the time. At one point, Tamara was so busy living out of a suitcase, traveling between cities, making presentations, and achieving the next goal, she never had an idle moment for herself. Even if she managed to find some margin in her schedule, she confessed, "I could be doing five other things with my time." That's when Tamara found herself stuck at the Newark, New Jersey, airport, which is notorious for delayed flights. And this delay was a doozy—six hours. But, as with J.K. Rowling, it opened up an important window of nonachievement.

"In that particular section of the airport where my gate was located, there weren't any outlets to charge your phone or computer and no televisions," Tamara recalled. "So you're just pretty much stuck sitting there for six hours thinking, watching people, or maybe reading."

The most valuable time that knowledge workers have is time to think. Tamara's team was then trying to redesign the billing system. The problem was that none of the proposals already floated would work. "We've done that before," someone would say before dismissing the idea. "None of the solutions we were coming up with represented fresh or innovative ideas," she said. "But being in that space sitting still for that amount

> **The most valuable time that knowledge workers have is time to think.**

of time, with not really anything to do, allowed an idea to surface."

Tamara came up with a way to restructure the billing system. Unlike previous suggestions, it was an approach they hadn't tried yet. "I hadn't even considered it before," she said. But thanks to the spare time, she hit on a solution. "That project ended up being a $10 million savings to the business," she said. Ten million dollars is a pretty remarkable payday for six hours of doing nothing.

So far we've seen how periods of nonachievement drive results. But these examples have been brought on by desperation or necessity. The next step is realizing that you can intentionally carve out time away from work to noodle on problems, think, puzzle, and dream. Which brings us to our client Roy.

Pause for Profit

Roy, who we introduced in chapter 4, is a very successful high-achieving national account manager within the home improvement sector. His parent company has 6,000 employees and $4 billion in annual revenue. He, like his dad before him, had invested several decades of his life with the company. He knew his business inside and out. A number of years ago, Roy was traveling 80 percent of the time. While most of his work was centered in middle Tennessee, he also had business in Knoxville, Chattanooga, and Huntsville.

Although he had scaled his business unit from $24 million to $40 million in three years, there was never a time when he didn't feel completely stressed out. "I was just a train wreck," he told us. "I wasn't present for my family. I wasn't present for work. I couldn't get it all done. So, yeah, I was not succeeding at life and winning at work." Keep in mind that Roy had twelve kids "on purpose"—seven biological children, and five whom he and his wife felt called to adopt, all at one time, out of a bad situation in Liberia.

Roy reached the point where he recognized he couldn't continue to scale the decisions he needed to keep everything running smoothly. "I needed a platform to train other people and a platform where I could have my growing team dump

Intentionally carve out time away from work to noodle on problems, think, puzzle, and dream.

everything about all the projects we were managing into one place."

The problem was, that platform didn't exist. As Roy puzzled on the problem, what Steven Johnson would call a "slow hunch" emerged.[10] So Roy, working with his son as the lead developer, decided to carve out some mental space apart from his regular duties to innovate a creative software solution. That tool helped him scale his business to almost $53 million in sales. His parent company took notice. Roy was going to sell the software in a public offering. But the company offered to buy it instead, and Roy's continued to make money on the system through integrations. "That software program idea came out of the space that I created for nonfocused work," he said.

Making White Space Official

White space can be deployed at the corporate level, although it rarely is. One notable exception was the way the leadership team at Google created more margin for engineers to dream and innovate without the guillotine of achievement hanging over their heads.

One day a week, 20 percent of their time, engineers are excused from pursuing their usual workload to explore whatever side project they want. No agenda. No expectations. No goals to achieve. Just a big, fancy sandbox of opportunity to play in. Sound crazy? Unconventional? Risky? Absolutely. Does it work? Yes. Exceptionally well.

According to one report, "In a typical year, more than half of Google's new offerings are birthed during this period of pure autonomy."[11] You might want to let that sink in.

For example, during his 20-percent free time, Google scientist Krishna Bharat created Google News, which currently attracts millions of daily visitors. Other innovations born out of the 20-percent free time include Gmail, Google Talk, Google Translate, and Google Sky.

We won't even attempt to calculate the dollar value to Google's bottom line from those apps. Alec Proudfoot, a Google engineer, observed, "Just about all the good ideas here at Google have bubbled up from 20 percent time."[12]

Naturally, Google still owns the intellectual property of anything that emerges during this weekly hiatus from their regular workload. Clearly, there's something extraordinary that happens when we step away from business-as-usual into the free-to-create nonachievement zone. Need more proof? Twitter, Slack, and Groupon all started as side projects.[13]

Nonachievement doesn't necessarily mean you're doing nothing at all. In all the cases we've seen, breakthrough ideas were a byproduct of being in a context where achievement wasn't the driving force, where the mind was given free rein to wander, imagine, innovate, and dream. This is what we mean when we say there's power in nonachievement.

Maintain a Hobby That Delights You

When our mutual friend Doug went through a health crisis, his doctor told him, "You need to take some time off. The stress of constant work is negatively affecting your health. You are not going to get well until you do." Doug protested: "But I love my work. It doesn't feel stressful to me."

His doctor explained what we've been exploring in this book—our brains and our bodies are not designed for constant work. We need breaks. We need to cultivate an intentional rhythm of work and rest. He then asked, "Do you have any hobbies?" Doug admitted he didn't.

This is a prime reason high achievers struggle with overwork and hitting the pause button. They simply don't know what to do with themselves if they're not working. "My work is my hobby," we hear from business owners we coach. It's no wonder you can find them during scheduled downtime on their laptop or phone instead of in the garden, stream, or kitchen; or on the green, trail, or field. Work is easier and, per chapter 2, more enjoyable and engaging than hobbies.

So, we have two leisure modes:

1. We take time off; feel weird, uneasy, and distractible; and then settle into something more comfortable: email, a spreadsheet, whatever.
2. Exhausted by our long hours, we struggle to engage with more meaningful pastimes and opt for thumbing down the bottomless feed of Instagram or vegging out while Netflix autoplays us into oblivion.

Those are extreme, but we've all experienced versions of both. It's possible to cultivate a sense of pure appreciation for simple nonachievement; for some that might be powerful enough to simply disengage from work. But others might require stronger medicine. Taking what we know from Mihaly Csikszentmihalyi's work on flow, the key is to cultivate hobbies and leisure activities that delight us.

Challenging, compelling, interesting hobbies bring enjoyment, as well as intellectual stimulation, which gives us something to invest our time and life in beyond our work. For those who have developed a love for cooking or gardening, they've discovered a tactile, sensory-rich experience that is very different from their day-to-day office work. And those who've made a hobby out of learning another language gain an appreciation for a culture different from their own.

Both of us enjoy fishing, especially fly-fishing. It's a generational thing in the Hyatt clan. Our fishing hobby has produced years of wonderful memories within our family. The challenge of placing a fly in just the right spot is thoroughly engrossing. And every time we cast a line, we're filled with peace, feel refreshed, and experience clarity. It's a centering routine, and we're both better leaders for it.

Plenty of research confirms the point. Not only do hobbies help renew the mind, one study found another benefit: "Spending more time on a hobby can boost people's confidence in their ability to perform their job well," as long as the hobby isn't similar to your profession.[14]

Researchers at San Francisco State University studied the impact on work performance that occurs when engaging in hobbies and creative activities such as cooking, photography, painting, and knitting. Assistant professor of psychology Kevin Eschleman reports, "We found that in general, the more you engage in creative activities, the better you'll do [at work]," and the study notes, "those who engaged in a creative hobby performed between 15–30 percent better at work."[15]

Hobbies aren't just a great way to improve your work performance. Research has found certain hobbies nourish your brain. Here are five hobbies and their benefits on the brain:

- Exercise improves long-term memory, decreases risk of dementia[16]
- Reading increases left temporal cortex brain connectivity[17]
- Learning a new language slows brain aging, improves later life cognition[18]
- Playing video games improves spatial navigation, strategic planning, motor performance[19]
- Playing a musical instrument enhances cognitive skills, verbal fluency, academic achievement[20]

It's no surprise that some of the greatest scientific minds in history understood the restorative benefits of practicing a hobby. Albert Einstein played violin, an instrument he taught himself. He sometimes played with Max Planck, who, when he wasn't busy developing quantum theory, enjoyed playing piano.[21] The newspaperman and critic H. L. Mencken also enjoyed piano and regularly played with a group of friends called the Saturday Night Club. He even wrote a comic opera.[22]

I (Michael) loved playing music as a teen. I played guitar in a rock band throughout my high school years and into college. I even played a regular solo gig at a bar outside of Waco, Texas. Sixty bucks a night plus all the beer I could drink.

At the end of my freshman year, a band from Austin invited me to play bass with them. This seemed like a big break. They asked me to drop out of college and move to a farm in Denton, Texas, where we'd rehearse until we could get on the road and make our fortune.

Somehow, my dad was okay with it. "This is the best time of your life to do that sort of thing," he said. "If it doesn't work out, you can always come back to school. But if it does work out, great! It's the dream job you've always wanted." I could barely believe my ears, but I packed my bags, slipped on my cowboy boots, and headed out the door. Trouble was, my bandmates wanted to smoke pot more than practice. I lasted six weeks before I called it quits. Dad wired me bus fare, and I headed back to civilization.

Since it was too late to return to college that semester, I took a job selling encyclopedias door-to-door. Dad always said sales was where you'd make the most money. I never made it in the music business, but I did leverage my selling skills to rise to the top of the book publishing business. In doing so, however, I made a bad trade-off of my own.

I ignored the musical side of my life for years as I climbed the corporate ladder. I didn't make margin for music even as a hobby. Two things changed that. First, as I discovered the power of the Double Win, I placed hard edges on my schedule. That freed up time for other pursuits. Second, knowing how much I loved music, Gail bought me two Native American flutes. Today, I own about ten flutes, all in different scales. Each is handcrafted from a variety of woods. And I've been taking lessons for several years now. I try to practice my hobby for twenty to thirty minutes a day.

It's worth pointing out that there's a potentially big hurdle for high achievers to overcome when starting a new hobby. That is the idea of going back to being a beginner, doing something you're not initially good at.

One of the big reasons people don't pursue hobbies or outside interests is because they are paralyzed by a limiting belief which says, "I'm not good at music," or "I didn't grow up with a dad who taught me how to fish," or whatever. The incredible thing about coaching is that somebody somewhere in the world already knows what you want to do and is available to help you figure it out—be that in-person or via a YouTube tutorial. When we're working on a new hobby and we're having to start at the very beginning, we're experiencing what it means to learn something for the first time. This fresh perspective brings a mindset to our business that can be very helpful.

You might be thinking, isn't there something more productive you could be doing with your time than maintaining a hobby? The answer is yes and no. You could always work more, pack the days and weeks till you can't find another second. But that's self-defeating, as we've already seen.

The most productive thing you can do is to be unproductive from time to time. Your body and mind will be better rested. You'll have more energy and better ideas. And you'll probably enjoy life more as well.

RETHINKING SLEEP

Rest Is the Foundation
of Meaningful, Productive Work

It is a very funny thing that the sleepier you are,
the longer you take about getting to bed.

C. S. LEWIS[1]

By her own admission, Tanya, one of our coaching clients, spent far too many years depriving herself of sleep—often clocking less than two hours a night. She's the CEO of a third-generation family business in the precision manufacturing industry. Her company machines parts, everything from screws that hold eyeglasses together to parts for no-failure industries like aerospace and medical devices.

Tanya has two highly active kids who were, at the time, involved in high school sports. Her daughter played club volleyball, which involved crisscrossing the country to compete at the top tournaments. To keep up with her daughter's road schedule while also juggling her responsibilities at the office, Tanya admitted she shortchanged her sleep for years.

"I convinced myself that I just didn't need any sleep because I needed to be on the road to support my daughter. And," she said, "I knew I could just schlep my work around with me in my backpack. I was a professional schlepper. I looked like a Teenage Mutant Ninja Turtle because my backpack was gigantic. I just sacrificed whatever it took to get the kids to where they had to go. And two hours of sleep was good."

Adding to the pressure she felt to win at work was the fact that "there are not a lot of women in manufacturing. I hang out with type A, hard-charging guys who are really successful. I didn't know if they slept, but I aligned with how they did things—and all of them were *always* on." She adds, "If that meant that I'd get only an hour and a half of sleep, then that's what I had to do. Most nights I couldn't shut my brain off. I just figured sooner or later my kids would be going to college and that's when I would sleep."

Complicating her situation was an overnight reversal on the balance sheet when a customer canceled their order due to bankruptcy. Her company went from a cash-positive position to a million-dollar cash-negative position. Tanya almost buckled under the weight of responsibility for her forty-two employees and the families they represented.

She had to find a way to turn the company around, which required more hours. "I attended everything, but I was always coming in at Mach 5 with my hair on fire. I didn't want to live that way, but I didn't know how *not* to be that way. Because I was both a mom and the boss, I fell into that Hustle Fallacy trap."

Tanya discovered she couldn't keep up that pace and continue to succeed. At the very time her company needed her best, she was unable to give it for lack of sleep. Many high achievers are learning this today as the research continues to mount, showing the rejuvenating power of sleep—and what happens when we don't get enough.

Good Sense Out the Window

"We're out of beer!" When you're seventeen, those four words present a crisis of sorts. Way back when, six friends and I (Michael) were drinking into the wee hours of Saturday morning. We had found the perfect spot on Lake Waco, a 79,000-acre man-made reservoir inside Waco, Texas, city limits. Free from adult supervision, it was the favorite watering hole for high school kids in town.

The crisis came around one o'clock in the morning. Nothing was open in those days past eleven at night, but one of our friends managed a nearby convenience store. "Guys," he announced, "the store is closed, but we've got beer in the cooler . . . and I've got the keys!" We all piled into my car, three in the front, four in the back, and drove into town.

After sneaking into the store, we grabbed a couple of cases of beer and headed back to resume our party. On the way to the lake, my friends got a head start on the beer. The windows were down. We were high-fiving each other and laughing at our success.

Then a police car came down the road. It slowed as the officer passed us. I looked in my rearview mirror at what he could see inside my car and started to sweat. No doubt seven guys drinking beer in a car at two in the morning might attract attention. It did. His car lit up like a Christmas tree a split second before he flipped a U-turn and started toward us. I'm not sure what came over me, but rather than pull over and await our fate, I punched the gas.

A mile later I made a hard left off the main road into a residential area, hoping to ditch the pursuing cop. While we darted up and down residential streets, my companions frantically tossed beer bottles out of the windows, hoping to get rid of all the evidence. They were about finished when I spotted a way out of the neighborhood. I made another sharp turn and floored it. Anticipating that move, however, two more police cars blocked the road. I came to a screeching stop.

Right then the officer with the light show pulled up behind me. He ran up to my door. "Everybody out!" he yelled. He was seething. He told us to put our hands against the car and spread our legs while he read us the riot act.

I decided to play dumb. "What's going on, Officer?" I said. "Is there a problem?"

"I could smell your beer from the moment I saw you till right now."

Gulp! "But," I objected, "we don't have any beer. We're clean."

He shook his head side to side and glared at me with eyes that would sober anyone. "I know exactly what you boys did. You were throwing those beer bottles out of your windows. Son, that's littering—on top of having an open container in a car, reckless driving, and avoiding arrest."

My heart sank like a rock. I was doomed. I saw my life pass before my eyes. But then our fortunes turned. "You boys are very lucky," he said, folding his arms. "We're cleaning out the jail tonight and don't have any room for you guys. Now, go on home and don't let me ever catch you pulling a stunt like that again."

Wait, *what?* He didn't haul us to the station? He didn't write me a ticket? He didn't even call our parents? He was letting us go with just a warning? I couldn't believe our luck.

I take no pride in my behavior that night. As youthful indiscretions go, it was a doozy. Looking back, I'm embarrassed by my lack of judgment. At the time, under the influence of a few beers, running from the cops seemed like a great idea. All the guys in the car were cheering me on as we raced away. But my judgment was impaired, to say the least. Why tell the story? Because many high achievers are in the same boat as my friends and me that night, functionally working with the judgment of an inebriant.

> **Many high achievers are functionally working with the judgment of an inebriant.**

Working Drunk

The health effects of skimping on sleep are well known: elevated stress hormones, reduced immunity, obesity, cardiovascular disease, diabetes, heightened risk of stroke, early death, and other undesirables. Less appreciated is the effect of poor sleep on our work performance.

How many hours of sleep do you get? A third of American adults get fewer than six hours of sleep a night, and even those reporting more might get less than they assume. We get fewer winks than we think because we tend to count time in bed, not time actually sleeping.[2]

What's the harm? Once a person pushes past seventeen, eighteen, nineteen, twenty hours without sleep, they might as well be drunk, displaying impairment approaching, even exceeding, the legal limit. And it's not hard to get there. Let's say you're up at 6:00 a.m. and stay up till midnight, catching up on a project or email and then Netflixing your favorite show before hitting the sack. That's eighteen hours.

"Many people remain awake for periods of 16 hours or more for reasons of work, family, or social life," concluded researchers A. M. Williamon and Anne-Marie Feyer after a study comparing drinkers to nonsleepers. "After this duration of wakefulness fatigue reaches a level that can compromise safe performance."[3]

The impact on our mental and emotional faculties is significant. Mood, memory, decision-making abilities, creativity, even IQ all suffer when we short our sleep. In fact, according to neuroscientist Tara Swart, when you lose a night's sleep, you're "operating as if you've got a learning disability."[4]

Achieving important company goals requires creative thinking and real-time problem solving. But innovation, pattern spotting, and lateral thinking all decline with insufficient sleep. The thought processes that allow those functions are powered by sleep and suffer without it. I (Megan) am worth nothing at work (or home) if I don't get at least eight hours a night. And the best way I (Michael) know to stay sharp all day is getting a quick nap right after lunch. Without sleep, our effectiveness goes down the drain. It's true for all of us.

According to neuroscientist Penelope Lewis, "Sleep-deprived people come up with fewer original ideas and also tend to stick to old strategies that may not continue to be effective."[5] Researchers can see why by looking at the brain. In 2017 a team of scientists discovered that neural activity declines in states of sleep deprivation. Our brain cells bog down and can't communicate with each other.[6]

Not surprisingly, we face other communication problems as our brains slow down. Whether we're talking about coworkers, friends, kids, spouses, anyone, we can't move through the world with other people unless we can regulate our emotions and understand the emotions of others. We have to, for instance, be able to read expressions and translate tones of voice. Poor sleep makes that problematic.

"In a sleep-deprived state, your brain is more likely to misinterpret these cues and to overreact to emotional events, and you tend to express your feelings in a more negative manner and tone of voice," write Nick van Dam and Els van der Helm in *McKinsley Quarterly*. They point to research showing sleep-deprived people struggle with trusting others, and that groggy bosses have less-engaged employees.[7]

Sleep deprivation undermines our ability to navigate the relationships that make our lives work. And we don't even know how bad off we are. When depriving ourselves of rest, we're less able to see how much it's costing us or why. The part of the brain where complex thought and reasoning reside is especially sensitive to overwork and insufficient rest. When our judgment is impaired, we can't admit or even notice that our abilities and capacities are also impaired. "The first part of your brain that turns off with sleep deprivation,"

When **depriving** ourselves of **rest**, we're less able to see how much it's **costing** us or why.

says Harvard professor Robert Stickgold, "is the little part that says, 'I'm not performing so well.'"[8]

Habitually shortchanging your sleep to meet deadlines, clear your inbox, or complete a project might earn you accolades from peers or a boss who commends you for doing the impossible. They, like my drinking buddies, might be cheering you on as the reds and blues flash behind you. The cult of overwork celebrates achievement, but it's too shortsighted to applaud the self-care practices that make achievement possible to begin with.

Big Boast, Small Truth

People brag about how much they work and play but never how much they sleep. Usually, it's the opposite. Celebrity executives, famous entrepreneurs, and their admirers tout their short nights under the covers as instrumental in their success.

We've encountered a couple of them in these pages already—Elon Musk and Martha Stewart—but the list could go on for pages: Jack Dorsey, Marissa Mayer, Indra Nooyi, Sergio Marchionne, Julie Smolyansky, Dominic Orr. . . . And people feel compelled to follow their lead.

In companies all over, bragging rights go to those who work the most and sleep the least. That's especially true in America where we work longer hours and rest less than practically anyone else in the world.[9]

David Dinges, who heads up the sleep and chronobiology division at the University of Pennsylvania, calls this celebration of restlessness "sleep braggadocio."[10] It's related to the humblebragging we talked about in chapter 2. In the cult of overwork, boasting about short sleep is another way of letting people know you're important. It's a signal you're adding value, that you're irreplaceable, which means it might also be driven by fear. If we close our eyes too long, we're worried we might be upstaged and replaced.

From where we sit, this all seems pointless. As historian Susan Wise Bauer says, "The larger the boast, the smaller the truth."[11] We shouldn't focus on what we might gain from incremental hours in front of our screens. Such gains are largely illusory. Given what we know about the high costs of sleeplessness, we should instead focus on the exponential losses we're suffering.

A study by Rand Europe found the US loses almost 3 percent of its total GDP each year because we skimp on sleep, more than any other country.[12] And *Forbes* writer Michael Thomsen says sleep-deprived thinking might be to blame for the high failure rate in Silicon Valley, a place that prizes workers who treat sleep the way vampires treat holy water.[13] In those kind of cultures, bad ideas last longer than they should and good people wash out, their health and families enduring the fallout.

Looking back at the company's launch, Facebook co-founder Dustin Moskovitz admits he would have been more effective if he hadn't deprived himself of proper rest and nutrition. "It is with deep sadness that I observe the current culture of intensity in the tech industry," he says. "My intellectual conclusion is that these companies are both destroying the personal lives of their employees and getting nothing in return."

Now the CEO of Asana, Moskovitz looks back on his sleepless days at Facebook with regret. With adequate sleep and proper nutrition, he says, "I would have been *more* effective: a better leader and a more focused employee. I would have had fewer panic attacks, and acute health problems. . . . I would have picked fewer petty fights with my peers in the organization . . . AND I would have been happier."[14]

Instead of shorting our sleep, the research indicates we should be investing in it. In fact, it's safe to say the Double Win is otherwise impossible. Sleep creates the necessary conditions for success in all domains of life.

Sleep More, Achieve More

There are a number of ways sleeping more at night helps us accomplish more during the day, both at work and at home. For starters, sleep keeps us sharp. How many times have you gone mentally blank in a meeting, nodded at your desk, or forgot where you were going? It's happened to us more than we'd like to admit.

As we've seen, skimping on sleep—even a little—can dramatically impair our mental performance, creating fatigue, inability to focus, slow reaction times, and more. A habit of good sleep, however, produces mental clarity, improved judgment and decision-making ability, and sharper memory.[15]

Sleep improves our ability to remember, learn, and grow. We're sure brainteasers are fine, but adequate sleep is the best learning tool there is. Our minds are particularly active when we sleep, integrating new information learned during the day, processing memories, and sorting the significant from all the meaningless stuff we pick up. This is known as "post-learning sleep."[16] Even dreaming is critical to this process. If our work depends on our creativity and insight—and whose doesn't?—then sleep is essential.

Sleep also refreshes our emotional state. Nothing can make us feel depressed, moody, and irritable like missing sleep. To press the reset button, just go to bed. Sleep reduces stress chemicals in the brain and helps us gain control of our emotions. "During REM sleep," writes Tom Rath, citing research from Berkeley, "memories are being reactivated, put into perspective and connected and integrated, but in a state where stress neurochemicals are beneficially suppressed."[17] The result is that we can start the day emotionally fresh and empowered if we invest in our sleep.

Finally, *sleep revitalizes our bodies.* We all have a body clock. When we ignore its signals and play longer or work more, we create unnecessary stress, and that stress contributes to depression, fatigue, weight gain, high blood pressure, and a lot worse. But sleep lowers the stress chemicals in our bodies, boosts our immune system, and improves our bodies' metabolism. Instead of waking unrested after putting in extra hours on a project, why not approach it recharged the next day? You'll do better work and feel better about it.

Cheating our sleep is like maxing out our credit cards.

Bottom line: we act like sleep is a luxury or an indulgence; as a result, sacrificing sleep in the name of productivity has become routine. But the opposite's true. Cheating our sleep is like maxing out our credit cards. There's a benefit now—at least, that's what it feels like—but the bill always comes due in the form of decreased mental ability and poor health.

The Daily Sabbath

In the last chapter we looked at the profitable pause. Though ebbing in some corners, we have natural breaks for resting and recharging embedded in our culture. The idea of a weekly sabbath is now millennia old and ensures we get time each week to disengage and rejuvenate. The idea goes back to the Genesis creation account when God rested on the seventh day.

But theologian Peter Leithart says we miss another, subtler reference to rest in the story of creation, and it's worth paying attention to, whether we're religious or not.

"There's another sabbath pattern that's built into the creation account," says Leithart. "It's not simply that God works full-time 24/6 for six days and then rests on the seventh day. There's a rest built in to every day."[18] How so? As Genesis conveys the action, God works during the daytime, but this work time is presented as the second half of the day. As the days are counted, evening comes first, and even now observant Jews reckon the new day starting at sunset, not sunrise. It's the same with the liturgical day in Orthodox Christian practice.

"The rest time precedes the work time," says Leithart. "And that gives us a clue for how we should think about sabbath and rest within our own lives. We're not simply working toward rest." It's not that we work so we can earn time off, time to sleep. We work because we have slept, because we are rested. "We're working out of a sense of rest," he says.

"It keeps us from being frantic, it keeps us from workaholism, because our work is done not scrambling so that we can get to the holiday. It's done out of a rest that's already achieved."[19]

That's why we should think of sleep, not as the reluctant end of one day, but the best way to start the next.

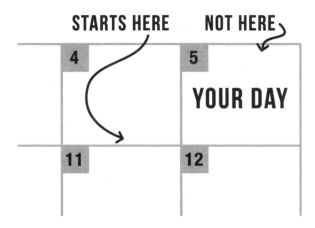

Start the Day
with a Good Night's Sleep

How much sleep do we really need? It varies person to person, but seven hours a night seems to be the minimum. Before artificial light, humans slept a lot longer than that. The best advice is to shoot for eight hours a night and see how you feel. It's not hard to clear the brain fog. One week of good sleep is all it takes to start feeling sharp again.[20]

Here's how we make sure we get a good night's sleep. No guarantees, but feel free to use and adapt these suggestions:

Prepare the environment. Make sure the room is dark. We pick up cues biologically from our environments. If it's dark, that cues us to go to sleep. "Room light," according to one report, "exerts a profound suppressive effect on melatonin levels and shortens the body's internal representation of night duration."[21] We use heavy block-out blinds and curtains to reduce outside light. And we dampen or eliminate light from tech in our rooms as well.

A cool room also helps. Chris Winter, president of Charlottesville Neurology and Sleep Medicine, says 65 degrees is the ideal temperature because "a cooler environment usually lends itself to a better quality of sleep."[22] Experts believe cooler temps help regulate our internal clock, which lowers our internal body temp while we sleep and raises it as morning approaches. Some experts say the ideal sleeping temperature is between 60 and 67 degrees. It's really a personal choice.

Run a fan or sound conditioner. About 5 percent of Americans use a "sound conditioner" or "sleep machine" at bedtime.[23] That percentage seems low to us. The white noise produced by a fan masks outside noise and helps us fall asleep and stay asleep. I (Michael) have been sleeping with a fan since college, and I (Megan) not only use a fan, but two white-noise makers! It's not overkill if you sleep well.

Prepare yourself. Avoid caffeinated drinks in the evening. Caffeine is a psychoactive stimulant that works against you at nighttime. When I (Michael) was younger, I could drink coffee anytime—even after dinner—and it didn't faze me at bedtime. No more. I cannot drink caffeine after 4:00 p.m. because it'll keep me awake until two in the morning. Everyone is different. If energy drinks are your thing, keep in mind some contain more than 300 milligrams of caffeine per can—three times the level in one cup of coffee.

Eliminate negative input, especially if you're a worrier by nature. When I (Michael) was the CEO of Thomas Nelson, we were owned by a private equity company in New York. This was in the middle of the recession, and I knew that if a call came after 7:00 p.m. from New York, there probably was a problem they wanted to discuss. I stopped taking those calls. I'd end up thinking about their issue all night and wouldn't get the necessary sleep for the next day. For you, it might mean avoiding the news or social media.

Listen to relaxing music. This doesn't work for everyone, but I (Michael) listen to the exact same music every night as I get ready for bed. It's become an audio cue that says to my subconscious mind and body, "It's time to go to sleep now." And while I like classic rock, I'd suggest building a calmer collection of tunes. Instrumental music is best, be it smooth classical, piano, or stringed arrangements. Gail and I have been listening to the same four or five songs every night for the last decade. I'm usually asleep by the middle of the second song. Having that kind of defined ritual helps.

Take a warm bath or shower. The bath is one of the best non-pharmacological methods of improving your sleep—and there's a ton of new research backing this up. Taking a relaxing bath is the centerpiece of my (Megan's) nightly routine. According to the findings of seventeen studies, "a bath or shower of about 104 degrees Fahrenheit before bedtime that lasted as little as 10 minutes was significantly associated with improved sleep quality, and increased the overall amount of time slept."[24] I'm in the tub no more than fifteen minutes, and it makes all the difference. The ideal time frame for a bath or shower is one or two hours prior to bedtime.[25]

Pray with your spouse. While this won't necessarily apply to all our readers, it's part of our bedtime routine and it works for us. Gail and I (Michael) pray together every night as we lie in bed. Joel and I (Megan) do as well. We pray about the things that are important to us, that concern us, or that we're dreaming about the future.

Beware sleep tracking. A word about sleep tracking tech is in order. Devices such as those offered by Apple Watch, Fitbit, Jawbone Up, Nike Fuel Band, and the like promise to quantify the length and quality of sleep. In theory, the data provides a "sleep score" with suggestions on how to optimize your sleeping routine. However, there's a growing body of research questioning the wisdom of using wearable sleep-tracking technology.

A study by the *Journal of Clinical Sleep Medicine* found sleep trackers might hurt more than they help by reinforcing "sleep-related anxiety or perfectionism for some patients."[26] This quest for the perfect night's sleep is known as *orthosomnia*.

Let's say you're the kind of leader who is obsessed with numbers at the office. You constantly study data with an eye on how to improve and beat your numbers from the last quarter. Nothing wrong with that. Here's the rub. When it comes to optimizing your sleep by fixating on improving your sleep number, you amplify your stress levels and end up making it harder to sleep.[27] Most sleep trackers aren't even that accurate.[28]

Finally, go to bed on time. If you're going to get a good night's sleep, you have to be disciplined to get to bed on time. This is still a struggle for us, but we have to be strict with ourselves. As high achievers, there's always one more thing to do, even if it's just one episode of our current favorite show.

We must resist the urge. If we're not careful, we think, *As soon as I finish this blog post . . .* , or *As soon as I get caught up on my messages. . . .* At some point, we have to draw a hard boundary and say, "Look, I'm going to bed on time because tomorrow is

---

GET A GOOD NIGHT'S SLEEP

- Prepare the environment
- Prepare yourself
- Beware sleep tracking
- Go to bed on time

important too. I'll be twice as efficient then. So rather than push a little longer, I'm going to get the rest I need now."

There's nothing wrong with doing more with less, but if we're not smart about our sleep, we can undercut our productivity and even our health. Instead of thinking of rest and sleep as self-indulgence, we need to think of them as self-improvement and the foundation of meaningful, productive work and life.

CREATING YOUR OWN DOUBLE WIN

Sometimes it's as if we're racing to the finish line our whole lives, skimming the surface and never dropping into life.

TARA BRACH[1]

Years ago, Gail and I (Michael) went to Maui to celebrate our anniversary. On the second day, we took snorkeling lessons. We started in the swimming pool, then progressed to the coral reef next to our hotel. We loved it. It was like swimming in a huge aquarium. Later that same day, we rented some snorkeling gear and determined that we would venture out on our own. We had discovered a new sport that we could do together.

The next morning, we made our way down to the beach. There wasn't another soul around. It was like a scene from *The Blue Lagoon*—pristine, tranquil, and stunning. We couldn't wait to get into the water. As we paddled about in the lagoon, facing down in the water, we were mesmerized by the aquatic life teeming just a few feet below us. We saw brightly colored fish, gently swaying plants, and, of course, the coral reef itself—alive with activity. It was truly a wow experience.

At some point, I decided to lift my head out of the water and look around. I gasped. The current had pulled us out to sea. The shoreline looked impossibly far away. Our hotel— all the hotels along the coastline—looked like toys in the distance. I immediately shouted to Gail who, fortunately, was still just a few feet from me. She looked up, saw our predicament, and then looked at me in near panic. "Oh my gosh! What are we going to do?"

Fortunately, we had a boogie board with us, on which we could place shells and other items we hoped to find on the ocean floor. We both grabbed on to it and started paddling for our lives—literally. We swam for more than an hour. Eventually, as we neared the shore, we stood up in the shallow water, trudged up to the beach, and collapsed on the sand, utterly exhausted.

We realized just how close we had come to disaster. This was not the outcome we had intended when we innocently slipped into the water that morning. You might say that the current conspired against us. We ended up at a place that we didn't choose or desire. Worse, we had lost our way, and unless we swam contrary to the forces working against us, we'd end up in grave danger out at sea.

A similar drift dynamic is at work in the lives of high achievers today. The cult of overwork is a powerful tide that can pull you far from shore if you're not aware of its force.

Even when we're aware of its power, we can still succumb to the current. But resisting should be somewhat easier now that you have five key principles to trade for the problem and practices to enable you to implement them.

The cult of overwork says

- work is the primary orientation for life;
- constraints stifle productivity;
- work-life balance is a myth;
- you should always be busy; and
- rest diverts time away from work.

But by now you know

- work is only one of many ways to orient your life, and you can define what winning at work and succeeding at life looks like for you;
- constraints foster productivity, creativity, and freedom, and you can constrain your workday;
- work-life balance is not a myth, and you can schedule what truly matters to you and those people most important to you;
- there's incredible power in nonachievement, and you can maintain nonwork activities that delight and rejuvenate you; and
- rest is the foundation of meaningful, productive work, and you can begin each day with a good night's sleep.

In other words, what you now know is that the Double Win is possible. You really can win at work and succeed at life. We've already explored how, but let's use this final chapter to dig in a bit more. We'll look first at what individuals can do and then broaden the scope to look at what employers can do.

What Individuals Can Do

When I (Megan) got sick with Crohn's disease, I had two surgeries and was in and out of the hospital for some time. During that period, it seemed like every time I turned around a nurse was jabbing me in the arm for an IV catheter or to take blood. I hated it.

That's when a dear friend and mentor who has had her own bout of health challenges told me about the butterfly needle. It was smaller than the normal needle and hurt less. I said I would feel silly asking for an accommodation like that, but my friend countered. "You should make this as easy on yourself as possible, Megan. There's no use making it harder than it needs to be."

WHAT INDIVIDUALS CAN DO

- Identify what you want
- Communicate what you want
- Arrange your life to get what you want

In her book *Bird by Bird*, Anne Lamott talks about being "militantly on your own side."[2] I pair Lamott's advice with my friend's all the time. Be on your own side. If it's harder than it needs to be, work to make it easier. And do so unapologetically.

We sometimes have a sort of "corporate Stockholm Syndrome" where we excuse and defend the culture of overwork in our companies and circle of friends.[3] We've got to stop working against ourselves. How? When it comes to what individuals can do, there are three primary steps we must take.

Identify what you want. Because of the drift dynamic mentioned above, we're often unaware of what overworking is or what it's costing us. It probably feels normal to most of us, at least once we've grown accustomed to that kind of punishment. It's just the water we're swimming in, the currents taking us where they will.

If you want the Double Win, you have to paddle against the current. That starts by getting clear on what the Double Win looks like for you. What does it look like for you to have a thriving professional life? What does it look like for you to have a thriving personal, family, and social life? Consider your non-negotiables. What does adequate—or even ideal—self-care look like to you? What are your relational priorities? Do you have the friendships you want? The relationship with your spouse you want? What about your

> **If you want the Double Win, you have to paddle against the current. That starts by getting clear on what the Double Win looks like for you.**

kids and extended family? What do you want to be responsible for at work? How many hours do you want to work each day?

What does winning look like to you in all of life's domains? To help you define your desires and put some shape to your aspirations, you might find it helpful to create a life plan and set annual goals. I (Michael) talk about that in my books *Living Forward* (cowritten with Daniel Harkavy) and *Your Best Year Ever*. The important thing to note is that progress always starts with desire and moves toward clarity. You don't have to have perfect clarity at the beginning. Clarity comes as you move toward what you want. But you have to know what you desire.

Communicate what you want. Unless you have extraordinary discretion over your time and money, you'll likely have others you're accountable to for how you use them. It could be your life partner or your business partner. It could be your board or your boss. It could be your clients or your team. It could be your customers or your vendors. Our lives are interconnected. Partners, bosses, clients, and the rest are also on their own side. To get what we want means we have to communicate and cooperate when possible.

This doesn't happen often at all. In one study of coping strategies in high-intensity jobs, 43 percent of employees acquiesce to overwork, while 27 percent pretend to go along with the culture of long hours. Only 30 percent were willing to advocate for changes to make their work fit the rest of their life and needs.[4] Of course there are risks in doing so, including potential pushback from unsupportive leadership, flak from acquiescent coworkers, possibly even fewer opportunities for advancement.

This will be especially challenging for people who identify as people pleasers or those who are conflict avoidant. We get it. But people pleasers ought, at the very least, to aim to please themselves. After all, they're people too. And if we're trying to avoid conflict, then we need to recognize that we're causing far more internal conflict than needed when we acquiesce to requests and demands that throw our work-life balance off-kilter.

It's never easy to draw new boundaries, renegotiate old deals, and redefine existing relationships, but it's necessary if we're going to experience the Double Win. We've already seen examples of professionals who've done that and succeeded—e.g., the P&G marketing manager in chapter 5 who restructured her hours, our own client Roy who convinced his higher-ups to leave him alone after-hours and let him keep delivering the results. It's possible. Either that or find or make a more accommodating job for yourself.

Arrange your life to get what you want. In my (Michael's) book *Free to Focus*, I talk about the Desire Zone. It refers to when you're working in areas of your greatest passion and proficiency. It's a simple concept: work is most enjoyable when you're great at what you do, and you love it too.

When we coach clients, we always encourage them to look for ways to eliminate, automate, or delegate anything that doesn't fit in their Desire Zone. It's not always possible, but the more discretion you have over your time and money, the more you can arrange your work to fit your interests and abilities. Sometimes we have clients who resist this, but after just minutes of troubleshooting, we help them identify ways they could move undesirable work off their plates. This has the benefit of enabling people to experience greater joy and satisfaction in their work.

This method also works well outside the office. It's important to recognize that maintaining a home is a full-time job. Even people without children can attest to the relentless demands.

To maintain reasonable work-life balance, two-income families have to either divide the burden and shoulder it themselves, or look for ways to eliminate, automate, and delegate parts of that job as well. Yard care, groceries, laundry, cooking, home cleaning and repair, and so much more can be outsourced, even on a budget. And this goes for single people, too, especially single parents.

So what would make it easier for you? Depending on your resources, you can find services and people to pick up just some of the burden or even all of it. Get intentional about eliminating, automating, and delegating what you can. You can't buy time, strictly speaking. But there are people and services who are eager to make a trade.

Ask yourself, what contributes more to your life: grocery shopping or napping? Folding laundry or riding bikes with your kids? Spending an evening out with your partner or cleaning house because you couldn't get to it over the weekend? Where is your passion and proficiency most utilized outside work? That's where you ought to be investing your nonwork hours.

What Leaders Can Do

When we talk about the Double Win, leaders often get excited. They're usually living the same horrifying statistics we've been looking at and suffering from the cult of over-work more than just about anyone. So when we talk about winning at work and succeeding at life, they're thrilled. It's like tossing a life preserver to a drowning person. People in desperate straits are usually unaware of the plight of others, and that can sometimes go for leaders. But once they've begun to break free from the cult of overwork, it's incumbent on them to liberate their teams.

We know, for instance, that rested employees are better employees. And it's almost impossible to separate work life and home life. When our personal lives suffer because of overwork, our work suffers too—or will eventually. Worst of all, burnout breeds cynicism. Thanks to lower productivity, it's not like overworked employees make any real gains for their sacrifices; rather, it's all about staying afloat in a dysfunctional work environment. This is a disaster waiting to happen, if it hasn't already. Not only does burnout hurt employees' professional and personal lives, it breeds the kind of cynicism that sours office culture and harms customer relations. When workers think success is zero-sum, and for the company to win, they have to lose, it's easy to turn septic and spread toxicity through the organization and beyond.

The surest defense against these problems is to empower your team to experience the Double Win for themselves. That always starts with the leader, because the leader must not only model the Double Win and champion it within and even outside the organization. But they are also the only ones who can change structural and policy-related reasons for overwork. There are many things that can be done to create a culture of the Double Win in your organization, but we want to recommend just five.

WHAT LEADERS CAN DO

- Model the Double Win
- Connect the dots for your people
- Give your team more autonomy
- Constrain the workday and workweek
- Resource your vision

Model the Double Win. The people who report to you, the people you work with, unconsciously begin to mimic you. Emulating is mostly unconscious and mostly inevitable, especially in relation to organizational leaders. People can't help it.

As a leader, you can't help it either. You're going to set the pace. If you work seventy hours a week, your people think they have to work seventy hours a week to satisfy you. You set the standard, and they believe unconsciously that's the standard they must keep.

The problem is, most of them are not going to be able to keep up, and you're going to be responsible for the consequences. If your marriage can handle it, great, but what if theirs can't? What if they go through a divorce, one of their kids goes off the rails, or their health is a bust? Are you willing to accept responsibility for that because as a leader you didn't exert the kind of influence that had a positive impact on people? I'm not, at least not anymore. The most

important thing you can do is model the behavior you want
to see:

- ► Multidimensional focus, not a myopic focus on work
  alone.
- ► A constrained workday and workweek, along with
  the creative thinking it fosters.
- ► Work-life balance.
- ► Intentional nonachievement and refreshing pastimes
  outside work.
- ► Sleep. No more emails at eleven at night.

Connect the dots for your people. We saw in chapter 4
that modern work requires us to make our own jobs to one
degree or another. This requires a lot of intellectual and even
emotional work for employees. That's especially true when
the company vision, goals, strategic priorities, and progress
toward key milestones are absent or management shrouds
them in secrecy.

For great employee performance, leaders should connect
the dots. Share the company vision and goals often. Discuss the strategy and show what role individual jobs play in
achieving the goals and turning the vision into reality. It's
also critical to publicly discuss progress, including financial
performance whenever and to whatever extent possible. All of
these have the function of reducing the amount of the job they
have to create for themselves. You've made it crystal clear.

Give your team more autonomy. Once they're clear on
the vision, goals, and strategy, there's no reason to hold the

reins in. Give your people as much autonomy over the scope and setting of their work as possible. "When employees have greater control over when, where, and how they do their work," say professors Erin Kelly and Phyllis Moen, "they are less stressed, report better health, and are more engaged in their work and committed to their jobs."[5]

> **Give your people as much autonomy over the scope and setting of their work as possible.**

At Michael Hyatt & Co., for instance, we're semi-virtual. We have an office but allow our employees to work offsite as much as needed. We also have unlimited paid time off and work with department heads to ensure that their teams are taking enough time off each year. We've never had one employee abuse the privilege.

Constrain the workday and workweek. If you've hired high performers, the only problem you might have is people overworking on their own volition. As a leader, you should limit this as much as possible, and that starts by limiting the workday.

One of the reasons for overwork mentioned in chapter 2 was sky-high expectations. These include expectations of ourselves, our bosses, and our customers. Outside of explicit directives to work all day, no expectation is more counterproductive than what Harvard Business School professor Leslie Perlow calls "the cycle of responsiveness."

It starts as reasonable requests fall outside regular work hours. Well-meaning employees accommodate these requests, signaling they are apt to field such requests again. "Once colleagues experience this increased responsiveness, their own requests expand," Perlow says. "Already working long hours, most just accept these additional demands—whether they are urgent or not—and those who don't risk being branded as less than committed to their work. . . . [M]ost people don't even notice that they are spinning their way into a 24/7 workweek."[6]

Leaders can work against this by formally constraining the workday and workweek. At Michael Hyatt & Co., we absolve any employee from fielding Slack messages or emails after the workday ends or on the weekend. We also actively discourage anyone from sending such messages during those hours. If emergencies arise, we text. But that's rare.

That means teammates don't ever have to monitor work once the working period is over because no work is happening. We have to be flexible and accommodate rushed projects or other emergencies from time to time, but the constrained workday ensures that overworking is actively discouraged by company culture and company policy.

And don't forget the question of how much to constrain the workday. Plenty of companies are experimenting with reduced hours and reaping rewards for trying. As mentioned in chapter 4, we have a six-hour workday at Michael Hyatt & Co. Some companies have tried a four-day workweek. Evidence continues to show the success of these experiments.[7]

Resource your vision. Finally, if your vision, goals, and strategy consistently require you to reach into your employees' margin, there's something wrong. And we don't mean with your vision. What's wrong is your resourcing. Periods of extra demands are normal. But as Perlow's cycle of responsiveness shows, extra demands can easily become normal workloads. And that's a fundamental issue.

Work-life balance is not a myth, but workloads and expectations are sometimes completely unreasonable and make it impossible. The vision of high achievers always outstrips their resources. What separates effective leaders from mere taskmasters is the wisdom to know how much they can ask of their people and enough appreciation to resource and invest in them as needed. Employee lives are not credit cards to fund ambitious plans.

The View from Here

Whether as individuals or organizational leaders, your future depends to one degree or another on the choices you make right now. You'll never be in a better position to effect that future for the better than you are today, than you are right now. If you wait until next month, next quarter, or next year to start making changes, it will only get harder.

No matter how frustrated you may feel in your present reality, you're not a victim. You aren't doomed to face the impossible choice between the Hustle Fallacy and the Ambition Brake. You can pursue the third way. And you have agency over your future; you can choose to improve any of the underattended or needful domains of your life. *Now* is the best time to get clear on where you want to be and take the incremental steps on the pathway to the Double Win.

As humans, we have the privilege of determining our legacy. We can decide how we want to be remembered. But this is not a single choice; it is a series of choices. Blaming our circumstances or other people—even when they are partly

You have agency over your future.

or almost totally responsible—only makes us *victims*. It robs us of our freedom and keeps us stuck. It's never too late to change course and make your life count.

Are you overwhelmed in your role as a high achiever? Are you in a job you hate, living for weekends you can't even enjoy because you feel the phantom buzz of your phone all day? Are you a workaholic who, by choosing to overwork, is neglecting your family? Are you out of shape or sick because you've chosen to deprioritize your health? Do you lack deep, meaningful friendships? Are you a stranger to your own children? Is your spouse weighing the option of a divorce?

Regardless of where you find yourself as you read these words, you don't have to stay stuck in the state you are in. We can't always choose what happens to us, but we can always choose how we respond. The first step is to own your specific situation and take responsibility for the choices that led to it. Only then can you begin to create, experience, and enjoy a different future.

> **We can't always choose what happens to us, but we can always choose how we respond.**

Here's a good way to illustrate the transformation that's possible if you commit to the Double Win. Gail and I (Michael) now are in a position to take thirty days off every summer. We call it our annual sabbatical. We completely unplug from the business. Unlike the way I operated when our kids were young, I don't get email or take phone calls. I made a decision to be fully present.

This particular summer, we traveled to Jackson, Wyoming, for several weeks of hiking, fly-fishing, breathing fresh mountain air, and taking plenty of naps. It was enormously rejuvenating. The last night before we left, Gail said to me, "I'd like to get up tomorrow morning and see the sunrise." We had been sleeping in, so we hadn't watched the sun set that corner of the sky ablaze even once.

I said, "What time do we have to get up?"

She smiled. "Four a.m. should get us there in time."

You've got to be kidding me, I thought. Instead, I was a trouper and said, "Okay, honey, let's do it." When morning rolled around, I was so tempted to hit the snooze button. If I had, I would have missed an incredible experience. After a stiff cup of coffee, we drove out to Jenny Lake, took the ferry to the west dock, and then climbed to Inspiration Point.

We arrived at the top, sat down on a rock, and were overwhelmed by the breathtaking view of Jenny Lake. The glass-like, blue-pastel water served as a canvas, reflecting the early morning sunrise like a mirror. Beyond the edge of the glacially carved lake, we had a panoramic view of the city of Jackson Hole. From our perch, we saw the Cathedral Group, a cluster of three 12,000-plus-foot mountains—Teewinot, Mount Owen, and Grand Teton—framing the lake with their majestic rock formations.

After several minutes of silence, Gail turned to me and said, "Babe, thank you so much for making this possible. Thanks for getting up early this morning." She took my hand and added, "Most of all, thanks for making me a priority. I feel so loved, and I'm so grateful for you and to God for the opportunity we have here today."

What a radically different conversation that was when compared to the conversation I shared at the beginning of the book. If you recall, twenty years ago Gail, through her tears, told me she felt hopeless and overwhelmed like a single mom. We've come a long way. Again, our life's not perfect. But it's substantially improved as a result of the choice we made to get off the treadmill and take the path leading to the Double Win.

Imagine a Better Future

In light of this, we'd like for you to imagine a different reality for yourself. The cult of overwork thrives when our imagination shrinks. The Double Win comes into view when we envision it. So imagine a day when your business is growing exponentially, but you aren't working more hours. In fact, you're working fewer hours. Can you see it? What does it feel like?

Imagine a day when you're able to take time off away from the business, completely unplugged for a full month, with the confidence that nothing will fall through the cracks at the office. How does that feel? Is the stress starting to melt away just a bit?

Now, imagine a day when you're winning at work and succeeding at life—a day when you're thriving in the business you dreamed of and enjoying the life you've always wanted. Remember, you're not going to drift to that kind of destination. You have to design it. Good intentions aren't good enough. What decisions do you need to make to move toward your desired outcome?

Why not start by saying goodbye to frantically hustling on the treadmill? Why not use today as the day to change the trajectory of your business and your life? Don't hit the snooze button. Get started on the path to winning at work and succeeding at life. As we can attest, the view is spectacular.

NOTES

Chapter 1: The Double Win

1. Rushworth M. Kidder, *How Good People Make Tough Choices*, rev. ed. (New York: Harper, 2009), 6.

2. Ann Burnett, as quoted in Brigid Schulte, *Overwhelmed* (New York: Picador, 2015), 45.

3. Andy Stanley, *The Principle of the Path* (Nashville: Thomas Nelson, 2008), 15.

4. Milja Milenkovic, "42 Worrying Workplace Stress Statistics," American Institute of Stress, September 23, 2019, https://www.stress.org /42-worrying-workplace-stress-statistics.

5. Patrick J. Sherrett, "Don't Overwork Your Brain," *Harvard Business Review*, October 27, 2009, https://hbr.org/2009/10/dont-overwork -your-brain.

6. John Ross, "Only the Overworked Die Young," Harvard Health Publishing, December 14, 2015, https://www.health.harvard.edu/blog/only -the-overworked-die-young-201512148815.

7. "Workplace Stress Continues to Mount," Korn Ferry, n.d., https:// www.kornferry.com/insights/articles/workplace-stress-motivation.

8. Meg Cadaoux Hirshber, "Why So Many Entrepreneurs Get Divorced," *Inc.*, November 1, 2010, https://www.inc.com/magazine/201011 01/why-so-many-entrepreneurs-get-divorced.html; Sylvia Smith, "Should Entrepreneur Divorce Rate Scare You," Marriage.com, September 12, 2017, https://www.marriage.com/blog/marriage-and-entrepreneurs/should -entrepreneur-divorce-rate-scare-you; Chirag Kulkarni, "The Toughest Job an Entrepreneur Has Is to Keep Their Marriage Together," HuffPost.com,

September 13, 2017, https://www.huffpost.com/entry/the-toughest-job
-an-entrepreneur-has-is-to-keep-their_b_59b97a37e4b02c642e4a1352.

9. Jeanne Sahadi, "Being CEO Can Kill a Marriage. Here's How to
Prevent That," CNN Business, July 25, 2018, https://www.cnn.com/2018
/09/30/success/ceo-marriage/index.html.

10. Emma Seppala and Julia Moeller, "1 in 5 Employees Is Highly
Engaged and At Risk of Burnout," *Harvard Business Review*, February
2, 2018, https://hbr.org/2018/02/1-in-5-highly-engaged-employees-is-at
-risk-of-burnout.

11. Ron Carucci, "Stress Leads to Bad Decisions. Here's How to Avoid
Them," *Harvard Business Review*, August 29, 2017, https://hbr.org/2017
/08/stress-leads-to-bad-decisions-heres-how-to-avoid-them.

12. Bryan Caplan, "The Idea Trap," EconLog, November 1, 2004,
https://www.econlib.org/library/Columns/y2004/Caplanidea.html.

13. Caplan, "The Idea Trap."

Chapter 2: The Cult of Overwork

1. Cited in Mihaly Csikszentmihalyi, *Flow* (New York: Harper, 1991),
143.

2. Daniel McGinn and Sarah Higgins, "One CEO's Approach to Managing His Calendar," *Harvard Business Review*, July 2018, https://hbr.org
/2018/07/one-ceos-approach-to-managing-his-calendar.

3. Yoon Ja-young, "Smartphones Leading to 11 Hours' Extra Work
a Week," *Korean Times*, September 2016, http://www.koreatimes.co.kr
/www/news/nation/2016/09/488_207632.html.

4. Jennifer J. Deal, "Always On, Never Done?" Center for Creative
Leadership, 2015, https://cclinnovation.org/wp-content/uploads/2020/02
/alwayson.pdf.

5. Derek Thompson, "Are We Truly Overworked? An Investigation—
in 6 Charts," *Atlantic*, June 2013, https://www.theatlantic.com/mag
azine/archive/2013/06/are-we-truly-overworked/309321.

6. John Maynard Keynes, "Economic Possibilities for Our Grandchildren" (1930), in Lorenzo Pecchi and Gustavo Piga, eds., *Revisiting
Keynes* (Cambridge: MIT Press, 2008), 23.

7. Bertrand Russell, "In Praise of Idleness," *Harper's*, October 1932,
https://harpers.org/archive/1932/10/in-praise-of-idleness. See also A. J.
Veal, *Whatever Happened to the Leisure Society?* (New York: Routledge,
2019), 79.

8. Quoted in Veal, *Whatever Happened*, 86.

9. Rutger Bregman, *Utopia for Realists* (New York: Back Bay, 2017),
134.

10. "The Futurists: Looking Toward A.D. 2000," *Time*, February 25, 1966, http://content.time.com/time/subscriber/article/0,33009,835128-1 ,00.html.

11. The company was later purchased by and absorbed into Thomas Nelson, as one of its trade imprints. Today it goes by the name W Publishing. Nelson itself was later bought by HarperCollins.

12. Ryan Avent, "Why Do We Work So Hard?" *1843*, April/May 2016, https://www.1843magazine.com/features/why-do-we-work-so-hard.

13. Avent, "Why Do We Work So Hard?"

14. Avent, "Why Do We Work So Hard?"

15. Edmund S. Phelps, "Corporatism and Keynes," in Pecchi and Piga, eds., *Revisiting Keynes*, 101.

16. Alain de Botton, *The Pleasures and Sorrows of Work* (New York: Panthcon, 2009), 30.

17. Mihaly Csikszentmihalyi, *Finding Flow* (New York: Basic Books, 1997), 30–32.

18. Csikszentmihalyi, *Finding Flow*, 31.

19. Csikszentmihalyi, *Finding Flow*, 49.

20. Csikszentmihalyi, *Flow*, 158.

21. Csikszentmihalyi, *Flow*, 159.

22. While people experience flow about half their working hours, Csikszentmihalyi's studies show they experience it only 18 percent during leisure activities. They find work more engaging, more challenging than their chosen leisure activities. Csikszentmihalyi, *Flow*, 159.

23. Tim Kreider, "The 'Busy Trap,'" *New York Times*, June 30, 2012, https://opinionator.blogs.nytimes.com/2012/06/30/the-busy-trap.

24. Florence King, "Misanthrope's Corner," *National Review*, May 2001.

25. Silvia Bellezza et al., "Conspicuous Consumption of Time: When Busyness and Lack of Leisure Time Become a Status Symbol," *Journal of Consumer Research* 44.1, June 2017, https://academic.oup.com/jcr /article/44/1/118/2736404.

26. Burnett, as quoted in Schulte, *Overwhelmed*, 44–45.

27. Jack Welch, as quoted in Jody Miller and Matt Miller, "Get A Life!" *Fortune*, November 28, 2005, https://archive.fortune.com/maga zines/fortune/fortune_archive/2005/11/28/8361955/index.htm

28. David Steindl-Rast, *Essential Writings*, ed. Clare Hallward (Maryknoll: Orbis, 2016), 111.

29. Kieran Setiya, *Midlife: A Philosophical Guide* (Princeton: Princeton University Press, 2017), 133–38.

30. Setiya, *Midlife*.

31. David Kestenbaum, "Keynes Predicted We Would Be Working 15-Hour Weeks. Why Was He So Wrong?" NPR, August 13, 2015, https://www.npr.org/2015/08/13/432122637/keynes-predicted-we-would-be-working-15-hour-weeks-why-was-he-so-wrong.

32. Russell, "In Praise of Idleness."

Chapter 3: Our Multifaceted Lives

1. Anne-Marie Slaughter, *Unfinished Business* (New York: Random House, 2016), *xvii*.

2. Michael J. Coren, "The Days and Nights of Elon Musk: How He Spends His Time at Work and Play," Quartz, June 8, 2017, https://qz.com/1000370/the-days-and-nights-of-elon-musk-how-he-spends-his-time-at-work-and-play.

3. Neer Varshney, "Elon Musk Getting Richer Faster Than Any Other Billionaire This Year," Benzinga.com, February 3, 2020, https://www.benzinga.com/news/earnings/20/02/15243207/elon-musk-getting-richer-faster-than-any-other-billionaire-this-year.

4. Elon Musk, interview with Bambi Francisco Roizen, "Elon Musk: Work Twice as Hard as Others," Vator.TV, December 23, 2010, http://vator.tv/news/2010-12-23-elon-musk-work-twice-as-hard-as-others.

5. Musk, interview with Roizen.

6. Ryan Nagelhout, *Elon Musk: Space Entrepreneur* (New York: Lucent Press, 2017), 46.

7. Elien Blue Becque, "Elon Musk Wants to Die on Mars," *VanityFair.com*, March 10, 2013, https://www.vanityfair.com/news/tech/2013/03/elon-musk-die-mars?verso=true.

8. Becque, "Elon Musk Wants to Die on Mars."

9. Zameena Mejia, "Elon Musk Sleeps Under His Desk, Even After a YouTube Star Raised $9,000 to Buy Him a Couch," cnbc.com, July 2, 2018, https://www.cnbc.com/2018/06/29/elon-musk-sleeps-under-a-desk-even-after-youtuber-crowdfunded-a-couch.html.

10. Coren, "Days and Nights of Elon Musk."

11. Sarah Gray, "A Shocking Percentage of Americans Don't Exercise Enough, CDC Says," Fortune.com, June 28, 2018, https://fortune.com/2018/06/28/americans-do-not-exercise-enough-cdc/.

12. Julia Horowitz, "Americans Gave Up Half of Their Vacation Days Last Year," *CNN Money*, May 25, 2017, https://money.cnn.com/2017/05/24/news/vacation-days-unused/index.html; Jessica Dickler, "Many US Workers Are Going to Lose Half Their Vacation Time This Year," CNBC, November 20, 2018, https://www.cnbc.com/2018/11/20/us-workers-to-forfeit-half-their-vacation-time-this-year.html.

13. Tara Kelly, "80 Percent of Americans Spend an Extra Day a Week Working After Hours, New Survey Says," Huffpost.com, July 7, 2012, https://www.huffpost.com/entry/americans-work-after-hours-extra-day -a-week_n_1644527.

14. Amy Elisa Jackson, "We Just Can't Unplug: 2 in 3 Employees Report Working While on Vacation," Glassdoor.com, May 24, 2017, https://www.glassdoor.com/blog/vacation-realities-2017.

15. Steven E. Landsburg, "The Theory of the Leisure Class," *Slate*, March 9, 2007, https://slate.com/culture/2007/03/an-economic-mystery -why-do-the-poor-seem-to-have-more-free-time-than-the-rich.html.

16. Robert Frank, "The Workaholic Rich," *Wall Street Journal*, March 21, 2007, https://blogs.wsj.com/wealth/2007/03/21/the-workaholic-rich.

17 *Atlantic* writer Derek Thompson calls this religion "workism." See his article, "Workism Is Making Americans Miserable," *Atlantic*, February 24, 2019, https://www.theatlantic.com/ideas/archive/2019/02 /religion-workism-making-americans-miserable/583441.

18. Charles E. Hummel, *Tyranny of the Urgent*, rev. ed. (Downers Grove, IL: InterVarsity Press, 1967), 4.

19. Richard Brookhiser, *George Washington on Leadership* (New York: BasicBooks, 2008), 167.

20. Amy Jen Su, "6 Ways to Weave Self-Care into Your Workday," *Harvard Business Review*, June 19, 2017, https://hbr.org/2017/06/6-ways -to-weave-self-care-into-your-workday.

21. Marcus E. Raichle and Debra A Gusnard, "Appraising the Brain's Energy Budget," National Institutes of Health, August 6, 2002, https:// www.ncbi.nlm.nih.gov/pmc/articles/PMC124895/.

22. Eva Selhub, "Nutritional Psychiatry: Your Brain on Food," Harvard Health Publishing, April 5, 2018, https://www.health.harvard.edu /blog/nutritional-psychiatry-your-brain-on-food-201511168626.

23. Sama F. Sleiman, "Exercise Promotes the Expression of Brain De-rived Neurotrophic Factor (BDNF) through the Action of the Ketone Body β-Hydroxybutyrate," National Institutes of Health, June 2, 2016, https://www.ncbi.nlm.nih.gov/pmc/articles/PMC4915811/.

24. David DiSalvo, "Why Exercising Your Legs Could Result in a Healthier Brain," *Forbes*, May 27, 2018, https://www.forbes.com/sites /daviddisalvo/2018/05/27/why-exercising-your-legs-could-result-in-a -healthier-brain/#61cbbd345235.

25. Ari Hyytinen and Jukka Lahtonen, "The Effect of Physical Activity on Long-Term Income," ScienceDirect.com, Social Science & Medicine, Vol. 96, November 2013, https://www.sciencedirect.com/science/article /abs/pii/S0277953613004188.

26. David Whyte, *Consolations* (Langley, WA: Many Rivers, 2015), 182.

27. Anne Fishel, "The Most Important Thing You Can Do with Your Kids? Eat Dinner with Them," *Washington Post*, January 12, 2015, https://www.washingtonpost.com/posteverything/wp/2015/01/12/the-most-important-thing-you-can-do-with-your-kids-eat-dinner-with-them/

28. Bronnie Ware, as quoted in Susie Steiner, "Top Five Regrets of the Dying," *Guardian*, February 1, 2012, https://www.theguardian.com/lifeandstyle/2012/feb/01/top-five-regrets-of-the-dying.

29. Ware, as quoted in Steiner, "Top Five Regrets."

Chapter 4: Liberation through Limits

1. Robert Keegan, *In Over Our Heads* (Cambridge: Harvard University Press, 1994), 154.

2. Kathleen Elkins, "Self-Made Millionaires Agree on How Many Hours You Should Be Working to Succeed," *CNBC Make It*, June 15, 2017, https://www.cnbc.com/2017/06/15/self-made-millionaires-agree-on-how-many-hours-you-should-be-working.html.

3. C. Northcote Parkinson, *Parkinson's Law* (Boston: Houghton Mifflin, 1957), 2.

4. Tonya Dalton, "How Many Hours Do You Really Need to Work Each Week to Be Productive?" *Fast Company*, June 25, 2019, https://www.fastcompany.com/90368052/how-many-hours-should-you-work-each-week-to-be-productive.

5. Erin Reid, as quoted in Sarah Green Carmichael, "The Research Is Clear: Long Hours Backfire for People and for Companies," *Harvard Business Review Ascend*, August 19, 2015, https://hbr.org/2015/08/the-research-is-clear-long-hours-backfire-for-people-and-for-companies.

6. Sara Robinson, "Why We Have to Go Back to a 40-Hour Work Week to Keep Our Sanity," AlterNet.org, March 13, 2012, https://www.alternet.org/2012/03/why_we_have_to_go_back_to_a_40-hour_work_week_to_keep_our_sanity.

7. Schulte, *Overwhelmed*, 139.

8. Keegan, *In Over Our Heads*, 154 (emphasis in original).

9. Keegan, *In Over Our Heads*, 152–53.

10. Phil Hansen, "Embrace the Shake," TED, February 2013, https://www.ted.com/talks/phil_hansen_embrace_the_shake.

11. Hansen, "Embrace the Shake."

12. Hansen, "Embrace the Shake."

13. Oguz A. Acar et al., "Why Constraints Are Good for Innovation," *Harvard Business Review*, November 22, 2019, https://hbr.org/2019/11/why-constraints-are-good-for-innovation.

14. Acar et al., "Why Constraints Are Good for Innovation."

15. Catrinel Haught-Tromp, as quoted in Tom Jacobs, "Constraints Can Be A Catalyst For Creativity," *Pacific Standard*, June 14, 2017, https://psmag.com/news/constraints-can-be-a-catalyst-for-creativity.

16. Alex Soojung-Kim Pang, *Shorter* (New York: Public Affairs, 2020), 177–79.

17. Pang, *Shorter*, 208.

18. Pang, *Shorter*.

19. Warren Buffett, as quoted in Amy Blaschka, "This Is Why Saying 'No' Is The Best Way To Grow Your Career—And How To Do It," *Forbes*, November 26, 2019, https://www.forbes.com/sites/amyblaschka/2019/11/26/this-is-why-saying-no-is-the-best-way-to-grow-your-career-and-how-to-do-it/#3355469479da.

Chapter 5: The Promise of Balance

1. Richard Sheridan, as quoted in Schulte, *Overwhelmed*, 124.

2. Steve Farber, "Why Work-Life Balance Is a Lie, and What Should Take Its Place," Inc.com, September 26, 2018, https://www.inc.com/steve-farber/work-life-balance-is-a-lie-heres-what-should-take-its-place.html.

3. Hosea Chang, "The Myth of Work-Life Balance," *Forbes*, January 3, 2019, https://www.forbes.com/sites/forbeslacouncil/2019/01/03/the-myth-of-work-life-balance/#4f2606443727.

4. Teresa Taylor, "Dispelling the Work-Life Balance Myth in Three Steps," *Huffington Post*, December 3, 2015, https://www.huffpost.com/entry/work-life-balance-myth_b_8085338.

5. Maria Popova, "Why We Lost Leisure: David Steindl-Rast on Purposeful Work, Play, and How to Find Meaning in the Magnificent Superfluities of Life," Brain Pickings, December 12, 2014, https://www.brainpickings.org/2014/12/22/david-steindl-rast-leisure-gratefulness.

6. Martha Stewart, as quoted in Jessica Lutz, "It's Time to Kill the Fantasy That Is Work-Life Balance," *Forbes*, January 11, 2018, https://www.forbes.com/sites/jessicalutz/2018/01/11/its-time-to-kill-the-fantasy-that-is-work-life-balance/#60d99f3970a1.

7. Walter Isaacson, *Einstein* (New York: Simon and Schuster, 2008), 367.

8. Myra Strober, *Sharing the Work* (Cambridge: MIT Press, 2016), 217.

9. Dick Costolo, as quoted in Pete Leibman, "A Fit CEO Is an Effective CEO: Why Leaders Need to Make Time for Exercise," Salon.com, September 9, 2018, https://www.salon.com/2018/09/09/a-fit-ceo-is-an-effective-ceo-why-leaders-need-to-make-time-for-exercise/.

10. Claire M. Kamp Dush et al., "Marital Happiness and Psychological Well-Being Across the Life Course," National Institutes of Health, May

10, 2013, https://www.ncbi.nlm.nih.gov/pmc/articles/PMC3650717/#R 28; Hyoun K. Kim and Patrick C. McKenry, "The Relationship Between Marriage and Psychological Well-Being: A Longitudinal Analysis," *Journal of Family Issues*, November 1, 2002, https://journals.sagepub.com /doi/abs/10.1177/019251302237296.

11. Aristotle, as quoted in Meg Meeker, *Raising a Strong Daughter in a Toxic Culture: 11 Steps to Keep Her Happy and Safe* (Washington, DC: Regnery Publishing, 2019), 11.

12. Mayo Clinic Staff, "Friendships: Enrich Your Life and Improve Your Health," MayoClinic.org, August 24, 2019, https://www.mayoclinic .org/healthy-lifestyle/adult-health/in-depth/friendships/art-20044860.

13. "A New Happiness Equation: Worker + Happiness = Improved Productivity," Bulletin of the Economics Research Institute 10.3, 2009, https://warwick.ac.uk/fac/soc/economics/research/centres/eri/bulletin /2009-10-3/ops/.

14. Jennifer Goldman-Wetzler, *Optimal Outcomes* (New York: HarperBusiness, 2020), 4.

15. Juliana Menasce Horowitz, "Despite Challenges at Home and Work, Most Working Moms and Dads Say Being Employed Is What's Best for Them," Pew Research Center, September 12, 2019, https://www .pewresearch.org/fact-tank/2019/09/12/despite-challenges-at-home -and-work-most-working-moms-and-dads-say-being-employed-is-whats -best-for-them/.

16. Eileen Patten, "How American Parents Balance Work and Family Life When Both Work," Pew Research Center, November 4, 2015, https:// www.pewresearch.org/fact-tank/2015/11/04/how-american-parents-bal ance-work-and-family-life-when-both-work/.

17. Juliana Menasce Horowitz, "Who Does More at Home When Both Parents Work? Depends on Which One You Ask," Pew Research Center, November 5, 2015, https://www.pewresearch.org/fact-tank/2015/ 11/05/who-does-more-at-home-when-both-parents-work-depends-on -which-one-you-ask/.

18. Schulte, *Overwhelmed*, 238–39. See also chap. 2, "Leisure Is for Nuns."

19. Schulte, *Overwhelmed*, 165.

20. Michelle P. King, *The Fix* (New York: Atria, 2020), 24–27. See also chap. 5 of Schulte, *Overwhelmed*, "The Ideal Worker Is Not Your Mother," 71–96.

21. Melanie Healey, as quoted in Joann S. Lubin, *Earning It* (New York: HarperBusiness, 2016), 142–43.

22. Judith Shulevitz, "Why Don't I See You Anymore?" *Atlantic*, November 2019.

Chapter 6: A Profitable Pause

1. Robert Poynton, *Do Pause* (London: Do Book Co., 2019). The epigraph is from the subtitle of the book.

2. J. K. Rowling, as quoted in Stylist Team, "The Big Idea: Bestselling Authors Reveal the Creative Secrets and Inspirations behind Their Greatest Books," Stylist.co, https://www.stylist.co.uk/books/famous-authors-reveal-the-ideas-and-inspiration-behind-their-best-selling-books-stories-creative-writing-influences/127082.

3. Amy Watson, "Number of the Harry Potter Books Sold in the United States and Worldwide as of August 2018," Statista.com, September 12, 2019, https://www.statista.com/statistics/589978/harry-potter-book-sales; "J.K. Rowling's 'Harry Potter' Translated to Scots, Marking 80th Language," NPR.org, November 23, 2017, https://www.npr.org/2017/11/23/566283284/j-k-rowlings-harry-potter-translated-to-scots-marking-80th-language; David Lieberman, "Harry Potter Inc: Warner Bros' $21B Empire," Deadline.com, July 13, 2011, https://deadline.com/2011/07/harry-potter-inc-warner-bros-21b-empire-146754; Emma Jacobs, "How JK Rowling Built a $25bn Business," *Financial Times*, June 26, 2017, https://www.ft.com/content/a24a70a6-55a9-11e7-9fed-c19e2700005f.

4. Shulevitz, "Why Don't I See You Anymore?"

5. Kevin J. Ryan, "A Day in the Life: Bayard Winthrop, 2/22/18," *Inc.*, May 2018, https://www.inc.com/magazine/201805/kevin-j-ryan/bayard-winthrop-american-giant-daily-routine.html.

6. "Work Email Onslaught: Staff Have Nowhere to Hide, US Study Finds," GFI Software, June 24, 2015, https://www.gfi.nl/company/press/2015/06/work-email-onslaught-staff-have-nowhere-to-hide-us-study-finds. Reference to time-diary studies comes from Shulevitz, "Why Don't I See You Anymore?"

7. Adam Waytz, "Leisure Is Our Killer App," *MIT Sloan Management Review*, Summer 2019, https://sloanreview.mit.edu/article/leisure-is-our-killer-app/.

8. Mihaly Csikszentmihalyi, *Creativity* (New York: Harper, 2013), 353–54.

9. Kreider, "The 'Busy Trap.'"

10. Steven Johnson, *Where Good Ideas Come From* (New York: Penguin, 2011).

11. Daniel H. Pink, *Drive: The Surprising Truth About What Motivates Us* (New York: Riverhead Books, 2009), 94.

12. Alec Proudfoot, as quoted in Erin Hayes, "Google's 20 Percent Factor," *ABC News*, May 12, 2008, https://abcnews.go.com/Technology/story?id=4839327&page=1.

13. Adam Robinson, "Want to Boost Your Bottom Line? Encourage Your Employees to Work on Side Projects," *Inc.com*, March 12, 2018, https://www.inc.com/adam-robinson/google-employees-dedicate-20-per cent-of-their-time-to-side-projects-heres-how-it-works.html.

14. Matthew Warren, "Spending More Time on Your Hobbies Can Boost Confidence at Work—If They Are Sufficiently Different from Your Job," Research Digest, October 7, 2019, https://digest.bps.org.uk/2019/10 /07/spending-more-time-on-your-hobbies-can-boost-confidence-at-work -if-they-are-sufficiently-different-from-your-job/.

15. Kevin Eschleman, as quoted in Jessica Stillman, "How Your Hobbies Impact Your Work Performance," Inc.com, May 6, 2014, https:// www.inc.com/jessica-stillman/how-your-hobbies-effect-work-perform ance.html.

16. Michael E. Hopkins et al., "Differential Effects of Acute and Regular Physical Exercise on Cognition and Affect," US National Library of Medicine, National Institutes of Health, July 26, 2012, https://www.ncbi .nlm.nih.gov/pmc/articles/PMC3374855/.

17. Julia Ryan, "Study: Reading a Novel Changes Your Brain," *Atlantic*, January 9, 2014, https://www.theatlantic.com/education/archive /2014/01/study-reading-a-novel-changes-your-brain/282952/.

18. Viorica Marian and Anthony Shook, "The Cognitive Benefits of Being Bilingual," Cerebrum, US National Library of Medicine, National Institutes of Health, September–October 2012, https://www.ncbi.nlm.nih .gov/pmc/articles/PMC3583091/.

19. S. Kühn et al., "Playing Super Mario Induces Structural Brain Plasticity: Gray Matter Changes Resulting from Training with a Commercial Video Game," US National Library of Medicine, National Institutes of Health, February 19, 2014, https://www.ncbi.nlm.nih.gov /pubmed/24166407.

20. Nancy Fliesler, "Does Musical Training Help Kids Do Better in School?", Boston Children's Hospital *Vector*, June 19, 2014, https://vector .childrenshospital.org/2014/06/does-musical-training-help-kids-do -better-in-school.

21. Perimeter Institute, "What Great Scientists Did When They Weren't Doing Great Science: Even the Most Brilliant Minds Need to Unwind," InsideThePerimeter.ca, July 16, 2014, https://insidetheperimeter .ca/what-great-scientists-did-when-they-werent-doing-great-science.

22. Terry Teachout, *The Skeptic* (New York: Harper, 2003), 169–72; Frederick N. Rasmussen, "Mencken, The Musical: The Sage's Other Side," *Baltimore Sun*, September 1, 2007, https://www.baltimoresun.com /news/bs-xpm-2007-09-01-0709010298-story.html.

Chapter 7: Rethinking Sleep

1. C. S. Lewis, *The Silver Chair*, chap. 4, collected in The Chronicles of Narnia (New York, Harper, 2004), 571.

2. Connor M. Sheehan et al., "Are U.S. Adults Reporting Less Sleep? Findings from Sleep Duration Trends in the National Health Interview Survey, 2004-2017," *Sleep* 42.2, February 2019, https://academic.oup.com /sleep/article-abstract/42/2/zsy221/5185637; Diane S. Lauderdale et al., "Objectively Measured Sleep Characteristics among Early-Middle-Aged Adults: The CARDIA Study," *American Journal of Epidemiology* 164.1, July 1, 2006, https://academic.oup.com/aje/article/164/1/5/81104.

3. A. M. Williamon and Anne-Marie Feyer, "Moderate Sleep Deprivation Produces Impairments in Cognitive and Motor Performance Equivalent to Legally Prescribed Levels of Alcohol Intoxication," *Occupational and Environmental Medicine* 57.10, October 2000, https://www.ncbi.nlm .nih.gov/pmc/articles/PMC1739867/pdf/v057p00649.pdf.

4. Tara Swart, as quoted in Katie Pisa, "Why Missing a Night of Sleep Can Damage Your IQ," CNN.com, April 20, 2015, https://www.cnn.com /2015/04/01/business/sleep-and-leadership/.

5. Penelope A. Lewis, *The Secret World of Sleep* (New York: St. Martin's Press, 2013), 18.

6. Yuval Nir et al., "Selective Neuronal Lapses Precede Human Cognitive Lapses Following Sleep Deprivation," *Natural Medicine* 23.12, November 6, 2017, https://www.ncbi.nlm.nih.gov/pmc/articles/PMC5720899.

7. Nick van Dam and Els van der Helm, "The Organizational Cost of Insufficient Sleep," McKinsey Quarterly, February 1, 2016, https://www .mckinsey.com/business-functions/organization/our-insights/the-org anizational-cost-of-insufficient-sleep.

8. Robert Stickgold, as quoted in "Get Sleep: Steps You Can Take to Get Good Sleep and Improve Health, Work, and Life," Harvard Medical School, 2013, http://healthysleep.med.harvard.edu/need-sleep/whats-in -it-for-you/judgment-safety.

9. Alex Soojung-Kim Pang, *Rest* (New York: Basic Books, 2018), 2.

10. David Dinges, as quoted by Tanya Basu, "CEOs Like PepsiCo's Indra Nooyi Brag They Get 4 Hours of Sleep. That's Toxic," *Daily Beast*, August 21, 2018, https://www.thedailybeast.com/ceos-like-pepsicos-in dra-nooyi-brag-they-get-4-hours-of-sleep-thats-toxic.

11. Susan Wise Bauer, *The History of the Medieval World* (New York: Norton, 2010), 22.

12. Larry Alton, "Why Lack of Sleep Is Costing Us Billions of Dollars," NBC News, June 2, 2017, https://www.nbcnews.com/better/better /why-lack-sleep-costing-us-billions-dollars-ncna767571.

13. Michael Thomsen, "How Sleep Deprivation Drives the High Failure Rates of Tech Startups," *Forbes*, March 27, 2014, https://www.forbes.com/sites/michaelthomsen/2014/03/27/how-sleep-deprivation-drives-the-high-failure-rates-of-tech-startups. See also Dan Lyons, "In Silicon Valley, Working 9 to 5 Is for Losers," *New York Times*, August 31, 2017, https://www.nytimes.com/2017/08/31/opinion/sunday/silicon-valley-work-life-balance-.html.

14. Dustin Moskovitz, as quoted in Marco della Cava, "Facebook Co-Founder Moskovitz: Tech companies risk destroying employees' lives," *USA Today*, August 20, 2015, https://www.usatoday.com/story/tech/2015/08/20/facebook-co-founder-moskovitz-says-tech-industry-destroying-personal-lives/32084685/.

15. Ruth C. White, "Secret to a Better Brain, Younger Face and Longer Life," *Psychology Today*, November 16, 2011, https://www.psychologytoday.com/us/blog/culture-in-mind/201111/secret-better-brain-younger-face-and-longer-life.

16. Erin J. Wamsley and Robert Stickgold, "Memory, Sleep and Dreaming: Experiencing Consolidation," National Institutes of Health, March 1, 2011, https://www.ncbi.nlm.nih.gov/pmc/articles/PMC3079906/.

17. Tom Rath, *Eat Move Sleep: How Small Choices Lead to Big Changes* (Arlington, VA: Missionday, 2013), 154.

18. Peter Leithart, "Daily Sabbath," Theopolis Institute, YouTube video, 2:40, December 2, 2019, https://www.youtube.com/watch?v=zndktJOJprk.

19. Leithart, "Daily Sabbath."

20. "Sharpen Thinking Skills with a Better Night's Sleep," Harvard Health, March, 2014, https://www.health.harvard.edu/mind-and-mood/sharpen-thinking-skills-with-a-better-nights-sleep.

21. Joshua J. Gooley et al., "Exposure to Room Light before Bedtime Suppresses Melatonin Onset and Shortens Melatonin Duration in Humans," *Journal of Clinical Endocrinology & Metabolism* 96, no. 3, March 1, 2011, E463–E472, https://doi.org/10.1210/jc.2010-2098.

22. Samantha Lauriello, "This Is the Best Temperature for Sleeping, According to Experts," Health.com, July 9, 2019, https:/./www.health.com/condition/sleep/best-temperature-for-sleeping.

23. Markham Heid, "5% of Americans Sleep with a 'Sound Conditioner,'" Time.com, June 4, 2019.

24. Susie Neilson, "A Warm Bedtime Bath Can Help You Cool Down and Sleep Better," NPR.org, July 25, 2019, https://www.npr.org/sections/health-shots/2019/07/25/745010965/a-warm-bedtime-bath-can-help-you-cool-down-and-sleep-better.

25. Ana Sandoiu, "When's the Best Time to Take a Warm Bath for Better Sleep?" Medical News Today, July 22, 2019, https://www.medical newstoday.com/articles/325818.

26. Kelly Glazer et al., "Orthosomnia: Are Some Patients Taking the Quantified Self Too Far?" *Journal of Clinical Sleep Medicine* 13.2, February 15, 2017, https://doi.org/10.5664/jcsm.6472.

27. Shannon Bond, "Losing Sleep Over the Quest for a Perfect Night's Rest," NPR Morning Edition, February 18, 2020, https://www.npr.org /2020/02/18/805291279/losing-sleep-over-the-quest-for-a-perfect-nights -rest.

28. L. J. Meltzer et al., "Comparison of a Commercial Accelerometer with Polysomnography and Actigraphy in Children and Adolescents," US National Library of Medicine, National Institutes of Health, August 1, 2015, https://www.ncbi.nlm.nih.gov/pubmed/26118555; Glazer et al., "Orthosomnia: Are Some Patients Taking the Quantified Self Too Far?"

Chapter 8: Creating Your Own Double Win

1. Tara Brach, as quoted in Schulte, *Overwhelmed*, 277–78.

2. Anne Lamott, *Bird by Bird* (New York: Anchor, 2019), 105.

3. James Ullrich, "Corporate Stockholm Syndrome," *Psychology Today*, March 14, 2014, https://www.psychologytoday.com/us/blog/the modern-time-crunch/201403/corporate-stockholm-syndrome.

4. Erin Reid and Lakshmi Ramarajan, "Managing the High-Intensity Workplace," *Harvard Business Review*, June 2016, https://hbr.org/2016 /06/managing-the-high-intensity-workplace.

5. Erin Kelly and Phyllis Moen, "Fixing the Overload Problem at Work," *MIT Sloan Management Review*, Summer 2020 issue, April 27, 2020, https://sloanreview.mit.edu/article/fixing-the-overload-problem -at-work/.

6. Leslie A. Perlow, *Sleeping with Your Smartphone* (Boston: Harvard Business School Press, 2012), 7–8.

7. See Alex Soojung-Kim Pang's *Shorter* for more on this topic.

THANKS

ritish philosopher Mary Midgley once said writing a book is "like being an ant crossing the road." It's a daunting task no matter how many times you've crossed the street before. One thing we've learned is that you only make it across with the help of others, all of whom deserve our thanks.

I (Michael) began this book with my wife, Gail, and she's the perfect person to start these acknowledgments. Gail has been an encouragement and support to me for more than forty years now. There's no way I could do what I do without her.

I (Megan) could say much the same thing about my husband, Joel. Life is a two-person job, and I can't imagine doing it without him.

Nor could either one of us imagine writing this book without him. Joel is a true genius and always takes our ideas and helps them reach their full potential. This book would not be what it is without his expert guidance.

We're grateful for the work of Bob DeMoss, who helped to shape the initial draft of the manuscript and interviewed several of our BusinessAccelerator® coaching clients. And to our clients—Tiffany Bailey, Roy Barberi, Paul Bispham, Kyle Coolbroth, Tanya DiSalvo, Tamara Mosley, Chris Niemeyer, and Amy Wine—thank you for sharing your stories so generously. All of our BusinessAccelerator clients deserve a special shoutout here; we're crossing this road together.

That's also true for our team at Michael Hyatt & Co.: Courtney Baker, Vickie Bierman, Mike "Verbs" Boyer, Susan Caldwell, Chad Cannon, Ora Corr, Aleshia Curry, Michele Cushatt, Trey Dunavant, Anna Edwards, Andrew Fockel, Natalie Fockel, Amy Fucci, Megan Greer, Jamie Hess, Brent High, Adam Hill, Marissa Hyatt, Jim Kelly, Elizabeth Lynch, Sarah McElroy, Renee Murphy, Erin Perry, Johnny Poole, Charae Price, Tessa Robert, Danielle Rodgers, Deidra Romero, Katherine Rowley, Neal Samudre, Jarrod Souza, Blake Stratton, Emi Tanke, Rebecca Turner, Hannah Williamson, Lawrence Wilson, Kyle Wyley, and Dave Yankowiak.

Many thanks to our publishing team: our agent and dear friend, Bryan Norman of Alive Communications, and everyone at Baker Publishing Group: Dwight Baker, Brian Vos, Mark Rice, Patti Brinks, and Barb Barnes (who might be the most patient editor in the business).

We should also mention several people who have led the way for us, starting with our business coaches: Daniel Harkavy, Dan Meub, Ilene Muething, and Dan Sullivan. Beyond these, we've both learned from countless writers, thinkers, friends, and others: Stephen Covey, Ian Cron, Jason Fried, Chalene Johnson, Patrick Lencioni, Jim Loehr,

John Maxwell, Stu McLaren, Bryan and Shannon Miles, Dan Miller, Cal Newport, Alex Soojung-Kim Pang, Brigid Schulte, Tony Schwartz, Andy Stanley, and many others.

If crossing the road is a daunting task, why do it? The primary impetus for writing this book is the same as the impetus for achieving the Double Win in the first place: our families.

For me (Michael), that's Gail and my daughters: Megan, Mindy, Mary, Madeline, and Marissa.

For me (Megan), that's Joel and Fionn, Felicity, Moses, Jonah, and Naomi.

The secondary impetus is for our team, our clients, and customers. We want all of you to achieve the Double Win as well. Hopefully, this book will help you on the way.

INDEX

Acar, Oguz, 84
achievement, 24, 35, 90–92, 119–21, 127, 132, 133, 147
agency, 111
Ambition Brake, 15, 27, 110, 172
American Time Use Survey, 106
anxiety levels, 63
Aristotle, 102
autonomy, to work team, 169–70
Avent, Ryan, 38–41

balanced lifestyle, 59. *See also* work-life balance
Bauer, Susan Wise, 148
Bharat, Krishna, 133
bodily movement, 62–63
boundaries, of workday, 92–93
Brach, Tara, 159
Brookhiser, Richard, 60–61
Buffett, Warren, 87
Burnett, Ann, 15, 45
burnout, 21, 167
busyness, 44, 45, 46, 121, 161

butterfly needle, 162

calendar, 66–67
Caplan, Bryan, 21
Cardone, Grant, 76
Centers for Disease Control and Prevention, 57
climbing the ladder, 35
communicating what you want, 164–65
competitive edge, 62
complacency, 84
constraints, 87–88, 161
    drive productivity, 23, 78, 85–87
    enable focus, 81–83
    foster creativity, 23, 78, 83–85
    reality of, 79–81
    on workday, 92
control, as narcissistic, 110
"corporate Stockholm Syndrome," 163
Costolo, Dick, 101
COVID-19 crisis, 82

creativity, 124
  and constraints, 23, 78, 83–85
  and sleep, 144
Crohn's disease, 46
Csikszentmihalyi, Mihaly, 42–43,
  107, 124–25, 135, 179n22
cult of overwork, 20–22, 25, 38, 52,
  120–21, 123, 147, 163
  escaping from, 48–50
  as powerful tide, 160–61
cycle of responsiveness, 170, 171

daily sabbath, 151–52
De Botton, Alain, 41
definable wins, 43
Desire Zone, 165
Dilbert (comic), 43
Dinges, David, 147
distributing demands, 99
divorce rates, 21
domains of life, 22–23, 56, 77, 86,
  111, 164
Don Draper ideal, 108–9
Double Win, 17–19, 111, 161
  defining of, 71–74
  five principles of, 22–27, 50
  identifying, 163–64
  and leaders, 166–72
  path to, 172, 176
Double Win practice, 71–74, 90–93,
  113–16, 134–38, 153–57
dreaming, 149

eating well, 61, 62
effectiveness. *See* productivity
Einstein, Albert, 99–100, 136
endurance, 62
energy, 62

enhanced performance, 86
Eschleman, Kevin, 136
"everydayathon," 15
exercise, 57, 61, 62–63, 136

family, 12, 55–56, 102, 105
Family Dinner Project, 64
Feyer, Anne-Marie, 144
Fishel, Anne, 64
flow
  in hobbies, 43
  in work, 42–43
Frank, Robert, 57
freedom, and constraints, 23
friendships, 102–3
Full Focus Planner, 114
Furnas, Clifford, 33–34
future, envisioning of, 66

Goldman-Wetzler, Jennifer, 105
golf, 103
Google, 132–33
Graham, Billy, 34

Hansen, Phil, 83–84
happiness, and productivity, 103–5
hard boundaries, 82
Harry Potter series, 118
Harvard Business School, 32
Haught-Tromp, Catrinel, 85
Healey, Melanie, 109
health, 12, 20, 101, 105
high achievers, 43–44, 172, 174
hobbies, 43, 56, 61, 134–38
"humblebragging," 45, 147
Hummel, Charles, 59

Hustle Fallacy, 14, 27, 53, 110, 141, 172

Hyatt's Corollary, 78, 82

ideal week, 114–16

"idea trap," 21

innovation, emerges from constraints, 84

Jackson Hole, Wyoming, 174–75

Jetsons (cartoon), 34

Johnson, Steven, 132

Journal of Clinical Sleep Medicine, 156

Keegan, Robert, 80

Kellogg School of Management, 123

Kelly, Erin, 170

Kenstenbaum, David, 48

Keynes, John Maynard, 32, 41, 48–49, 57, 105

Kidder, Rushworth, 11

King, Florence, 44–45

King, Michelle, 108

knowledge workers, 79–80

Korea Labor Institute, 31

Kreider, Tim, 44, 127

Lamott, Anne, 163

leaders, and Double Win, 166–72

learning a new language, 136

leisure, 107, 123, 135

Leithart, Peter, 151–52

Lewis, C. S., 139

Lewis, Penelope, 145

life

arrangement of, 165–66

as multidimensional, 23, 53

LifeScore Assessment tool, 74

Loehr, Jim, 103

margin, 122–23

marital breakdown, 17, 21, 52

Maslow's hierarchy, 41

Mayo Clinic, 102

Mencken, H. L., 137, 171

Michael Hyatt & Co., 15–16, 26, 65, 82, 86, 125, 170–71

Moen, Phyllis, 170

Moskovitz, Dusti, 148–49

music, 154–55

musical instrument, 136

Musk, Elon, 51–54, 71, 76, 120, 147

negative feedback loop, 21–22

nonachievement, 24, 90–92, 117–33, 161, 169

nonnegotiables, 59–67, 77, 127, 163

Office, The (TV show), 43

on-the-job stress, 20

orthosomnia, 156

overwork, 20–22, 25, 32, 97, 120

as constant temptation, 38

health cost of, 101

reasons for, 38–48, 111

relational cost of, 102

and technology, 32

Pang, Alex Soojung-Kim, 86–87

Parkinson's Law, 78, 82

pause button, 134

Perlow, Leslie, 170–71

personal reflection, 61
Pew Research Center, 106
Phelps, Edmund, 41
Planck, Max, 136
Popova, Maria, 97, 98
"post-learning sleep," 149
Poynton, Robert, 117
priorities, 59
productivity, 23, 78, 79, 85–87,
    103–5
professional athletes, 103
professional class, working hours,
    57
professional results, 59, 65–67
profitable pause, 125, 151
Proudfoot, Alec, 133

Rath, Tom, 150
reading, 136
Reid, Erin, 79
relational priorities, 59, 63–65
relationships, 123
relaxation, 57, 125
rest, 24–25, 62, 63, 90–92, 99, 121,
    161
rested employees, 167
restlessness, 147
restorative activities, 88, 122
Robinson, Sara, 80
Rowling, J. K., 117–19, 129
Russell, Bertrand, 32–33, 49

sabbath, 151–52
sabbatical, 173
San Francisco State University, 136
saying "no," 87
Schulte, Brigid, 106, 107
Schwartz, Tony, 103

self-care, 59, 60–63, 123, 147
self-enrichment, 105
self-reflection, 127
Selhub, Eva, 62
Setiya, Kieran, 48
Sheridan, Richard, 95
shorter workday, 82–83, 86
sky-high expectation, 46–47
Slaughter, Anne-Marie, 51, 106
sleep, 25, 61, 62, 69, 139–52, 153–57
"sleep braggadocio," 147
"slow hunch," 132
social media, 45
"sound conditioner," 154
SpaceX, 51
Stanley, Andy, 17
status, 44–45
Steindl-Rast, David, 47
Stewart, Martha, 97, 108, 147
Stickgold, Robert, 147
stress, 20, 44–45, 63, 103, 125
Strober, Myra, 100, 105
Su, Amy Jen, 61
succeeding at life, 17–19, 161. See
    also Double Win
success
    as multidimensional, 23
    as zero-sum, 167
Swart, Tara, 144
Sweeney, Anne, 72
Switchfood (band), 69

technology, saddles with more over-
    work, 22, 32
Tesla, 51
"This is Your Life" (song), 69
Thomas Nelson Publishers, 12, 81
Thompson, Derek, 181n17

Thomsen, Michael, 148
time-out, 125–28
time to think, 129
treadmill effect, 47–48

University of Warwick, 103

vacation, 57, 88
value-signaling, 44–45
van Dam, Nick, 145
van der Helm, Els, 145
Vaynerchuk, Gary, 76
video games, 136

wandering mind, 123–24
Ware, Bronnie, 65
Waytz, Adam, 123
Welch, Jack, 47
wellness. See health
white noise, 154
white space, 122–23, 132
Whyte, David, 63
Williamson, A. M., 144
winning at work, 16–19, 161. See
    also Double Win
Winter, Chris, 153
women
    and work-life balance, 105
    workplace pressures of, 24
Word Publishing, 34

work
    disengaging from, 122
    expands and contracts, 77–78
    as fun, 38–41
    goodness in, 97
    only one dimension of life, 22–23,
        53–56
    personal growth and identity in,
        41–42
    as a religion, 59
workaholism, 17, See also overwork
workday
    constraint on, 170–71
    creating hard edges around, 78
    workism, 181n17
work-life balance, 23–24, 95–112,
    113–16, 169
    as dynamic, 99–100
    as intentional, 100–101
    not a myth, 20, 23, 25, 97–98,
        161, 172
    not same as rest, 99
    requires tension, 110
    trade-offs in, 101–5
workweek, constraint on, 170–71

Yale Center for Emotional Intel-
    ligence, 21

Michael Hyatt is the founder and chairman of Michael Hyatt & Co., which helps leaders get the focus they need to win at work *and* succeed at life. Formerly chairman and CEO of Thomas Nelson Publishers, Michael is also the creator of the *Full Focus Planner* and a *New York Times, Wall Street Journal*, and *USA Today* bestselling author of several books, including *Free to Focus, Your Best Year Ever, Living Forward*, and *Platform*. His work has been featured by the *Wall Street Journal, Forbes, Inc., Fast Company, Businessweek, Entrepreneur*, and other publications. Michael has been married to his wife, Gail, for more than forty years. They have five daughters, three sons-in-law, and nine grandchildren. They live just outside Nashville, Tennessee. Learn more at MichaelHyatt.com.

Megan Hyatt Miller is the chief executive officer at Michael Hyatt & Co. She is also the cohost of the Lead to Win podcast, which is consistently featured in the Top 100 in Apple podcasts. As the architect of Michael Hyatt & Co.'s standout culture, she is committed to helping her team win at work and succeed at life, while also delivering phenomenal results to their customers. Under her leadership, the company was named as one of *Inc.* Magazine's Best Workplaces for 2020, which ranks the top companies in America for their employee engagement. When she's not taking the company to new heights, she's fully present at home with her husband and five kids outside Nashville, Tennessee.

LEADING WITH VISION
CHANGES EVERYTHING

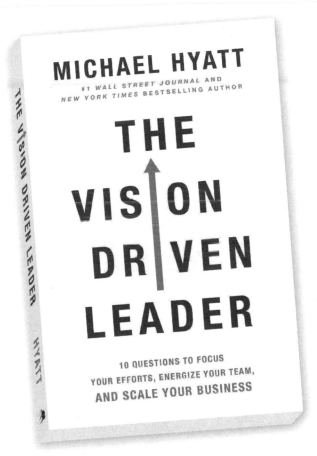

THE VISION DRIVEN LEADER

MICHAEL HYATT
#1 WALL STREET JOURNAL AND
NEW YORK TIMES BESTSELLING AUTHOR

THE
VISION
DRIVEN
LEADER

10 QUESTIONS TO FOCUS
YOUR EFFORTS, ENERGIZE YOUR TEAM,
AND SCALE YOUR BUSINESS

HYATT

How do you craft a vision? How do you get others on board? And how do you put that vision into practice at every level of your organization? Michael Hyatt asks ten simple questions to help you

- craft an irresistible vision for your business
- ensure it's clear, inspiring, and practical
- rally your team around the vision
- distill it into actionable plans that drive results
- overcome obstacles and pivot as needed

Slay Distractions, Reduce Your Task List,
AND FREE YOURSELF FROM INTERRUPTIONS

Reinvent your productivity with a total productivity system proven to help you reclaim hours of your workweek while achieving more.

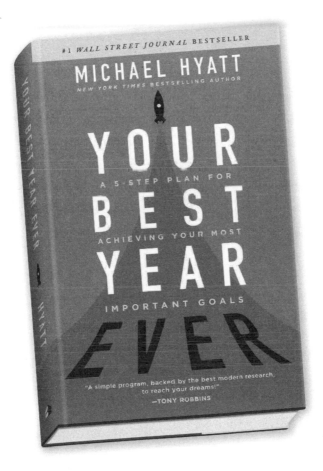

DESIGN A **MEANINGFUL LIFE**
OF **SIGNIFICANCE**

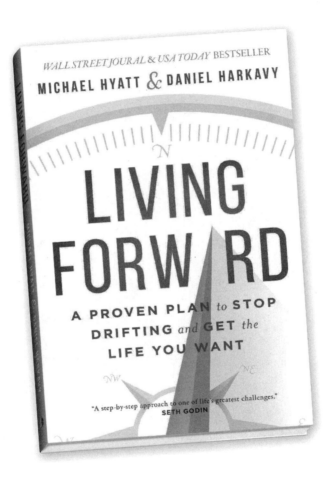

Build a Life Plan to help you stop drifting and create the life you want.

The Road to a Great Life Starts Here

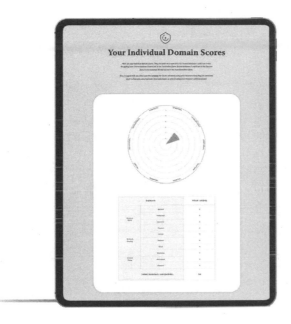

Before you can build a life that excels in every area that matters, you must first understand which life domains hold you back.

With Michael Hyatt's free **LifeScore™ Assessment**, you'll discover:

- ⊘ How well you're doing in your ten life domains
- ⊘ Which domains are keeping you from transforming your life from good to great
- ⊘ How to expand your strengths while improving the life domains that have fallen behind

When you've finished the assessment, you'll have the clarity you need to win at work and succeed at life.

Go to MichaelHyatt.com/Lifescore to get started →

Focus on What *Matters Most*

Say goodbye to the neverending to-do list that leads nowhere. The Full Focus Planner is Michael Hyatt & Co.'s bestselling physical planner to help you set goals and focus on the work that matters.

Plan your annual goals.

Break them up into weekly objectives.

Set daily targets to stay productive & focused.

GO TO **FULLFOCUSPLANNER.COM** TO CHOOSE THE PLANNER THAT FITS YOUR LIFESTYLE.